AIR FRYER COOBKOOK

AIR FRYER

COOKBOOK

MORE THAN **75** EASY RECIPES TO BAKE, GRILL, FRY, AND ROAST WITH YOUR AIR FRYER

FoxChase
HOUSE

The mission of Foxchase House is to publish great, quality, practical, and informative books that help you simplify your life. Our pride comes from the excellent job of our editors and the positive feedback from our fantastic community of book testers.

First edition published November 2019

ISBN: 978-1-7067-6623-0

Air Fryer Cookbook is a book published by Foxchase House Publishing

CONTENTS

INTRODUCTION

Some people might try to tell you that the air fryer is just another gimmick, but I'm here to tell you that it's not. An air fryer is a wonderful machine that can give you those divine potato chips and that perfectly cooked chicken with a crispy skin that you so crave, but without the excess oils and trans-fats that everyone dreads. The air fryer uses very little oil, or sometimes no oil at all, and can still create the same crispness and taste you get from a frying pan or deep frying your food. The air fryer is also light on electricity, can reduce your cooking time, and takes up very little space. It is a convenient, easy to use machine, and can do wonders to change and improve the way you prepare your meals forever.

1

THE MAGIC THAT IS THE AIR FRYER

The air fryer is a wonderful invention that was developed in England in 2008 but became popular worldwide at a very fast rate because of its ability to create delicious, crispy food simply, quickly, and in a very healthy way. The air fryer uses a concept similar to a convection oven, with a heating element and a fan to distribute the heat. Within the frying basket, your ingredients are heated evenly from all sides, and with the special pan attached to the basket, all the moisture and fats released by the cooking process can be gathered safely and without a big mess.

In general, there are two main methods of cooking food, namely dry heat and wet heat. Dry heat cooking uses mainly heat to crisp the outside of the food while using the natural moisture in your ingredients to steam them from the inside, and wet heat cooking uses boiling liquids to cook and steam ingredients from all directions. The most common dry heat methods are baking, roasting, and frying, and wet heat methods include cooking, poaching, and deep-frying. The air fryer is the ultimate tool for dry heat cooking as it fries food perfectly, and although the results won't be exactly the same, the air fryer is great for baking and roasting as well.

THE MAILLARD REACTION

The secret to how the air fryer manages to give food that heavenly crisp is something called the Maillard reaction. All ingredients, both plant-based and meat-based, contain copious amounts of amino acids, which are a key element in proteins, and reducing sugars, which are often used as natural reduction agents in chemical reactions.

When these amino acids and reducing sugars are exposed to intense heat, a chemical reaction occurs that rearranges them into rings, and these rings into groups. It's this chemical reaction that causes food to get that lovely brown color and crunchy texture, and also the heavenly new taste.

Exactly how the Maillard reaction alters your food is affected by many different elements, starting with the ingredients themselves. Different foods all contain their own types of proteins and natural sugars that will release their own unique aromas and flavors when exposed to the Maillard reaction. Another element is the intensity of the heat used to induce the Maillard reaction, as well as how long your food is exposed to the heat. Simply put, the higher the temperature you use to cook your food, the faster and stronger the reaction, and the longer you cook your food, the longer the reaction will continue.

It's important to know that exposing your food to extremely high temperatures, or continuously exposing it to heat for too long, can activate a completely different chemical reaction commonly known as "burning". Although charing your food a little bit can add an extra layer of flavor, too much of a burn can leave your meal tasting dry and bitter. Another big element to consider is moisture. When food is very wet, the water lessens the maximum heat the food will reach, and it will slow down the Maillard reaction a lot. That's why meat that is boiled will taste, smell, and look very different than meat being fried in a frying pan. Oil and butter are ingredients that conduct heat very well and strengthen the Maillard reaction a great deal, which is why they are used for pan-frying and deep-frying food. What makes the air fryer so great is that it manages to use the Maillard reaction to its fullest, without the aid of lots of oil and other fats.

WHY YOU SHOULD GET AN AIR FRYER

As mentioned, the air fryer is a great tool to improve the way you prepare food, and there are several reasons why you should consider buying an air fryer if you don't already own one.

1. The air fryer is a much healthier way of preparing food. Because the air fryer uses intense heat that is distributed equally, a much smaller amount of oil or butter is needed to get that lovely crispiness, and if you don't mind cooking your food for an extra few minutes, you don't need any oil or butter at all. This means that your general intake of oils and trans-fats will drop, which can help you live healthier in general, lessen the risk of cholesterol, obesity, and fat-related heart diseases, and even lose weight. The air fryer is a much healthier alternative to deep-fried foods, but if you prefer to cook with oil, the healthiest option is still to limit your intake of oily foods.
2. The air fryer is fairly inexpensive, especially compared to traditional or convection ovens, making it a great buy for anyone moving into a new apartment or starting a new household. It is still advisable to pay a little more for a good quality brand, as it will last longer and save you large amounts of money down the road in terms of repairs and replacements. Not only is the appliance itself fairly low cost, but it's also inexpensive in the long run. The air fryer is easy to maintain and uses little electricity, especially the models that require little to no preheating. A smaller model is a great buy for someone who is single, as you don't need a full-sized oven, which is expensive and heavy on electricity, to cook a meal for one person. As a bonus, you'll also save a lot of money on cooking oil etc., which you'll be using in smaller amounts for every meal.
3. The air fryer is very user-specific and can be bought to suit your needs. There are several sizes of air fryers on the market, as well as more or less complex models, various basket types, and even different colors. With a little bit of research and shopping, you can find an air fryer perfectly suited to what you need and want.
4. The air fryer is fairly compact and easy to move. Even the larger models of air fryers don't take up that much space, making them great for small kitchens. What makes them even better is that it's easy to move an air fryer around in the kitchen, as all you need is a flat surface and a power outlet. This makes the air fryer a great tool to take with you on vacation to areas where you might not always have access to other cooking implements.
5. The air fryer is very simple and easy to use and maintain. The air fryer tends to have simple, straightforward settings for both time and temperature, and some models even have preset modes for various functions for different food types, such as grilled chicken, french fries, frozen french fries, and roast beef. This makes it even more simple and easy to use, especially for beginners. The

separate parts of an air fryer are also designed to come apart easily, which makes them more convenient to wash. They are also treated with a non-stick coating to prevent grease and burnt food from sticking to the basket or pan.

6. The air fryer is very safe to use and is designed to minimize the risk of burning yourself. The entire cooking system is closed, meaning there's no risk of being splattered with hot oil or burning yourself on a hot frying pan or stove plate. The appliance also seals all heat inside, and with most models the basket and pan have a safe, heat resistant handle that never comes into contact with any heat. This lowers the danger of burning yourself even more.

7. Another great advantage of the air fryer is that you only use one appliance for all your cooking needs. With just the air fryer and the right basket, you can cook your entire meal without the mess of dirty dishes all over the place. What makes it even more convenient is that you don't need to constantly tend to the food while it's cooking, so you can prepare side dishes, set the table, and go about your business while you let the air fryer do its thing. There are also a myriad of different types of baskets, pans, and other accessories, each with their own functions, that can make your air fryer even more versatile and convenient, and better suited to your specific needs.

BUYING AN AIR FRYER

When shopping for an air fryer, it's important not to just walk into the store and but the first air fryer you see. There are dozens of different brands and models out there, and you need to put in the effort to find the right air fryer to match your specific needs. The first step is to do some research on the different brands. Look at the reviews of different air fryer brands on various websites to find out which brands of air fryer are the most reliable and trustworthy, and which brands should be avoided. Checking reviews can help determine which have issues and problems, as well as the level of quality to expect from the different brands since reviews are a good source of honest and fairly trustworthy information. For the best overview of the different brands, you should look at a large amount of both positive and negative reviews from various websites. Don't let just one or two reviews sway your opinion.

Once you've figured out which brands you can trust, it's time to put some thought into what you want out of your air fryer. The exact use you have in mind for your air fryer will have a great influence on the exact model of air fryer you should consider buying. A good example of one of the things to consider is whether you'll be cooking for a large family or just yourself. For big meals to feed the whole family, you'll need a large air fryer model with enough space, while a smaller model is much more suitable and cost-effective for a young bachelor cooking small meals for himself.

Another element to consider is how frequently you will use the air fryer. If your intention is to have your air fryer act as your main cooking implement and you're going to use it on a daily basis, it's advisable to go for a high quality, heavy-duty model and brand capable of keeping up with the hard work. If you plan to use your air fryer less often and only want a healthier way to cook up some french fries or jalapeno poppers every once in a blue moon, you can get away with a slightly lower quality, cheaper brand and model. The types of food you want to cook also have an impact and will determine which type of basket is most suitable. To cook a large variety of foods, you should look for an air fryer with a wider range of temperatures and lots of predetermined settings to make your life simpler and easier when it comes to cooking.

The most important element to keep in mind is your budget. Whether your budget is big or small, you have a limit to how much you're willing to pay for an air fryer, and you should look around among the different brands and models you've decided on. Your available funds will definitely influence the size, brand, and model of your air fryer. It's very important to shop around at different stores to find the cheapest prices or special offers, and you can even shop online for a good quality, reasonably priced air fryer. It never hurts to be cautious and careful when it comes to your funds.

Once you've chosen and bought your air fryer, it's time to accessorize. There are dozens of different types of separately sold attachments for your air fryer, such as baskets, pans, dividers, etc. all designed to make your cooking experience that much better. Once again, your intended purpose for the air fryer is key in your selection process. If you're going to spend a lot of time baking with your air fryer, you should look into specialized cake and muffin pans designed to fit into your air fryer. Oven racks are a good idea if you're thinking of roasting food and letting it rest while still keeping it warm. Dividers are great for if you want to bake your potatoes, fry your chicken, and roast your veggies at the same time. Some companies have even started adapting other supplies such as baking paper, etc. to be used together with your air fryer. There are even special racks available for toasting bread.

A very important thing to always check on is whether or not a specific accessory will work together with your specific size, model, and brand of air fryer. Most of these accessories will indicate which types of air fryer they are compatible with on the packaging, but if they don't, you should ask a store clerk or technician for assistance. Some other basic accessories, such as heat resistant tongs, pan liners, and thermometers should also be bought together with your air fryer to help your first attempt to cook with it run as flawlessly as possible. If you are new to the air fryer experience and don't have a specific plan in mind for how you want to use it, you should stick to the basics to begin with, and look into more specialized accessories once you've developed a better feel for how you want to work with your air fryer.

AIR FRYER BASICS

Now that you own an air fryer, the first, and most important, step is to read your user manual properly. The manual will guide you through the basic setup of your air fryer and walk you through all its functions, how to use it, and what you should do to get started. Read the manual thoroughly, and make sure you understand everything. Once you're done, store the manual somewhere safe, so that you can always go back to the manual when you face a problem in the future. These manuals often also come together with a few basic recipes, which are always a good thing to keep on hand.

The manual is a very important guide, but here are some basic tips and hints to help you with your air fryer:

- Before using your air fryer for the first time, wash it thoroughly to remove any dust and chemicals that may have come from the packaging and sales process. You should also wash all the parts of your air fryer if you haven't used it for an extended period of time, as it may have gathered dust along the way.
- Whenever you try to use your air fryer, take some time to prepare the basket, pan, or grates you plan on using. Although these items usually have a non-stick coating, there is still the risk of your food sticking to the pan. Use a little butter or oil to grease your pan, and avoid aerosol cans, as they often contain chemicals that are harmful toward the coating. Another alternative is to use liners such as aluminum foil or baking paper. Many brands have started selling these products shaped to fit your air fryer, with tabs to make it easier to remove your food once you're done cooking.
- Buy a small spray bottle to fill with oil. Many recipes require a small amount of oil to help your food get that extra bit of crisp, and a spray bottle is a great

way to coat your food evenly, with the minimal amount of oil and almost no effort.

- Greasy foods, such as fatty meat, bacon, etc. don't require any extra oil to get crispy. In many cases, the excess grease that drips into the bottom of the air fryer will start to boil and burn, resulting in white smoke leaking out of your air fryer. This is a very common occurrence and isn't a sign of problems with your air fryer. A simple way to get rid of the smoke is to pour a little bit of water into the air fryer before cooking, or to place a slice of bread on the bottom, to absorb all the grease. This will also help make it much easier to clean your air fryer afterward.
- Although most air fryers don't need it, preheating your air fryer for two or three minutes can help you reduce your cooking time. Some air fryers come with a preheat setting, but if yours doesn't, simply turn it up to the right temperature a few minutes before you're ready to start cooking your food.
- When preparing large amounts of food, cook your ingredients in batches, rather than all at once. If your air fryer is too crowded, the heat won't reach the middle of the cooking space properly, and your food won't cook and crisp evenly.
- Another way to help your food crisp evenly is to turn it halfway through the cooking process. The air fryer will pause all its functions whenever it's opened while still cooking and will continue when it's closed again. Use a pair of tongs to turn larger pieces of food like steak and chicken. For smaller types of food, such as french fries or chopped veggies, simply give your basket a good shake.
- Many people find that adding the suggested oil or butter halfway through the cooking process rather than beforehand helps the food become crispier. You can do this while you turn your food, and this is where that spray bottle will also come in handy.
- Whenever you're cooking frozen ingredients, always make sure to remove any ice that formed to get rid of any extra moisture. If any ingredients need to be soaked, rinsed, or marinated, make sure to properly pat them dry using a piece of paper towel, as extra moisture will result in your food being less crispy. A good indicator of too much moisture on or in your food is steam leaking out of the air fryer while you're cooking your food.
- It's very easy to use other cooking implements like metal bowls and muffin trays together with your air fryer, as long as these implements can withstand the high temperatures and fit comfortably inside the basket of your air fryer. Always make sure that it will be easy to remove these implements without burning yourself before you start cooking.
- Some meats, like steak, chicken, and pork, require a constant, steady internal temperature. For cases like this, it's very useful to have a quick read thermometer to help you monitor that internal temperature.
- As with an oven or microwave, it isn't wise to turn up the temperature in your air fryer higher than the recipe suggests. Despite what you might think, a higher temperature won't always flawlessly decrease your cooking times. In

most cases, your food will end up being burnt on the outside and raw on the inside.

- With some ingredients, such as french fries, a good way to reduce your cooking time is to put them in the microwave on high until they are halfway cooked, and then pop them in the air fryer for half the time just to get that lovely crispy exterior.
- When working with potatoes, it often happens that they are still hard after you've finished cooking them according to the recipe. This problem is usually caused by the potatoes themselves: some potatoes are just unusually hard from the start. A good way to soften potatoes before you start cooking them is to soak them in water for a few hours. The potatoes will absorb enough water to soften up a little, but not enough to interfere with their crispness when you fry them. This works great for when you're making fresh french fries, and if you're using whole potatoes, make sure to make a few small cuts so that the potatoes can absorb the water properly. Soaking the potatoes will also help remove any excess starch. Remember to pat your potatoes dry before putting them into the air fryer.
- Working with food items that don't have a lot of weight to them can be risky. Because of the strength of the fan the air fryer uses, things like small pastry squares or egg roll wrappings tend to fly around inside the air fryer as soon as it's turned on. There is a big chance that these can fly up into the fan and cause damage to your air fryer, so it's best to keep them away from your air fryer.

Although each recipe will give you the right temperature and cooking time, it sometimes happens that you just quickly want to throw something into the air fryer without following a specific recipe. To help you with that, here's a simple chart with the general cooking temperatures and times for the most commonly used ingredients:

INGREDIENTS	AVERAGE COOKING TIME	COOKING TEMPERATURE
French fries (thin, frozen)	12 – 16 min	390 ℉
French fries (thick, frozen)	12 – 20 min	390 ℉
French fries (thin, fresh)	15 – 20 min	400 ℉
Potato wedges	15 – 25 min	400 ℉
Vegetables (fresh)	15 – 25 min	350 ℉
Vegetables (stuffed)	10 min	320 ℉
Chicken nuggets	6 – 10 min	390 ℉
Chicken wings	16 – 22 min	360 ℉
Chicken breast	10 – 15 min	360 ℉
Drumsticks	18 – 22 min	370 ℉
Pork chops	15 – 20 min	355 ℉
Spare ribs	18 – 25 min	410 ℉
Hamburger	9-18 min	355 ℉
Steak	12 – 18 min	355 ℉
Fish sticks (frozen)	10 – 15 min	390 ℉
Spring rolls	12 – 18 min	390 ℉
Cheese Sticks (frozen)	10 – 15 min	355 ℉
Cake (in cake pan)	20 – 25 min	320 ℉
Muffins (special muffin pan)	15 – 18 min	390 ℉
Quiche (in cake pan)	20 – 22 min	355 ℉

RECIPE COMBINATIONS

One of the most useful accessories you can buy for your air fryer is a divider. This is a simple tool that lets you divide your air fryer basket into two or more sections, depending on the type. This means that you can cook several dishes at once, like roast and veggies, chicken and french fries, or fish and baked potato. It's fairly easy to combine different air fryer recipes, and the only definite rule is that the different recipes require the same cooking temperature. The cooking time isn't a problem, as you can simply remove the one dish as soon as it's done, and return the basket to the air fryer to continue cooking the rest of your meal. If you want both dishes to finish cooking at the same time, simply calculate the difference between the two cooking times. Let the recipe with the longer cooking time cook for the duration of that calculated difference, then add the second dish and cook for the full time the recipe for that dish requires. Both dishes should be perfectly cooked and ready to serve once the timer runs out.

Recipes with only a slight variation in temperature (such as 185 °F and 200 °F) can still be combined, as long as you adapt the cooking time to ensure all your food is properly cooked. There is no precise formula to determine how you should adapt your cooking time. You can only discover this through experimenting, and with time you'll develop a natural instinct for this. You should also spend a lot of time experimenting with different combinations and recipes, and you should explore the various options and recipes available to you as much as possible.

BASIC AIR FRYER SAFETY

Although the user manual will warn you about certain risks and inform you of how to use your air fryer safely, here are some more risks concerning the air fryer and important guidelines to help you stay as safe as possible.

A frequently overlooked hazard with most electrical appliances is the electrical elements being exposed to water. Never submerge the air fryer in water, and always make sure to keep the cable and plug away from all moisture. This is especially important when cleaning the exterior of the air fryer. Wet electrical wires are the fastest way to cause a short circuit and damage your air fryer or start a fire. The plug and cable should also be kept away from sources of heat to keep the protective casings for the electrical wires from melting and to prevent the wires from overheating and bursting into flame. If any of the electric wiring in the cable is exposed, using insulation tape is a very good quick fix, but you should have it properly repaired as soon as possible.

Another great risk is the excessive use of oil. The air fryer is designed specifically to work with small amounts of oil and too much oil can cause a fire. This is why you should always make sure not to pour too much oil over your food, and under no circumstances should you ever pour oil into the air fryer. Fires caused by heated oil are extremely dangerous and very difficult to put out.

The air fryer has several inlets and outlets to properly manage the airflow within the appliance. Covering any of these areas can not only affect the quality and condition of your food but can also cause serious damage to the air fryer. Your user manual should indicate where these inlets and outlets are, and you should always make sure that they aren't covered at all times.

The basket and pan of the air fryer are extremely hot immediately after use, and you should always be careful when handling them. When turning the food halfway through the cooking process or removing the food from the basket afterward, always make sure to hold the basket only at the handle and keep well away from any parts of the pan and basket that may have been exposed to heat. It's also a good idea to use tongs to remove the food from the basket rather than tipping the basket over. When washing the basket and pan of your air fryer, you should let them cool down for at least half an hour, as they will still be hot to the touch. You also shouldn't put them in water immediately after use, as the intense heat that will create has the ability to cause serious burns as soon as the implements make contact with the water. Children and pets should always be kept away from the air fryer at all times, whether it's still cooking your food, cooling off, or not in use at all.

A good extra precaution to take is to unplug the air fryer whenever it isn't in use. Not only will it keep a child from accidentally turning on the air fryer or from someone forgetting to turn it off, but keeping it unplugged will also protect your air fryer from damage caused by sudden electrical surges. Remember to always turn off the power outlet before you unplug the air fryer to protect yourself from electrical shocks.

This may seem a little redundant, but when you buy an air fryer, make sure to keep your payslip and warranty papers somewhere safe. Most air fryers come with a guarantee and warranty, and if you want to make a claim if something is wrong with your air fryer, you will need to provide the payslip. A good idea is to keep your payslip and warranty papers together with your user manual, to make sure you know exactly what they're for, and exactly where to find them.

CLEANING AND MAINTAINING AN AIR FRYER

In order to use your air fryer safely for years to come, it's important to take good care of it. The air fryer is relatively clean, especially compared to deep frying implements, but it's still critical that you clean your air fryer after every use. None of the parts of the air fryer are dishwasher safe, but luckily they are very simple and easy to clean. If you're cooking several dishes at once and plan to use the air fryer several times for one meal, you can simply leave off cleaning until you're completely done cooking the entire meal.

1. As mentioned before, it's important to unplug your air fryer and let it cool down properly before you start cleaning. Starting to clean while the air fryer is still hot will result in burns, and an air fryer still plugged into the outlet is hazardous.
2. Cleaning the outside of your air fryer is simple and easy. Simply use a damp cloth or sponge to wipe off any dust and dirt. Be careful not to use too much water, as the water could leak into the air fryer and cause damage. If for any reason, there is tough grime on the outside of your air fryer, it's alright to put in some elbow grease and use the abrasive side of the sponge.
3. To clean the basket and oil pan, use hot water and dishwashing soap. You can use either a sponge or cloth, but be careful not to use the abrasive side of the sponge. The basket and pan are covered with a non-stick coating, which is very easy to scratch. That is also why you should never use any metal appliances to remove food from the air fryer. If there are some bits of food stuck to the pan or basket, simply soak them until the bits soften, and then wash. Remember to rinse off the soapy water and make sure that both implements are completely dry before putting them back into the air fryer.
4. You can clean the inside of the air fryer with a damp cloth or sponge. Once again, be careful not to damage the non-stick coating. In the unlikely event of some crumbs or food bits sticking to the heating element of the air fryer, use a soft brush to brush the crumbs off and continue cleaning.

Aside from cleaning your air fryer, you should also take care of it when you're not using it. How and where you store your air fryer can have a large effect on how long and how well it will work. Always store your air fryer upright in a dry space. Keeping it on the countertop is fine, as long as you keep it dry and free of dust. Some air fryer models have built-in compartments for their cables, and it is always wise to store your cables safely in their compartment. As mentioned in the safety section of this book, never leave your air fryer plugged in if it's not in use. Even if you don't use your air fryer regularly, you can still keep it stored on your countertop as long as you give it a good dusting every now and then. Just be sure you clean off any accumulated dirt and dust before using it.

Along with proper cleaning and storage, here are some more basic maintenance tips to keep your air fryer up and running for as long as possible:

- The first, and most important, thing to do is to always stick to the user manual. The instructions provided are created with your precise model in mind for the purpose of keeping you safe and your air fryer working in prime condition. Always turn to your manual if you are unsure about something or come across any problems.
- Along with the cables, you should inspect every individual element of your air fryer for any form of damage or problems. Any damage to any part of your air fryer can potentially be harmful towards both you and your air fryer.
- Before you use your air fryer, you should always inspect the cables for any exposed or damaged wiring. If you come across any damaged wiring, don't use your air fryer, and make a plan to bring it in for repairs as soon as possible. A good way to protect your wiring from damage is to avoid twisting and unnecessary bending as much as possible when storing your cables.
- Make sure that your air fryer is always clean and clear of any dust before you use it. Be especially sure that there isn't any dust in the inlets or outlets. Dust can very easily clog the outlets and cause serious damage to your air fryer. The inside of your air fryer should also be properly cleaned on the inside, to make sure your food is hygienic and clear of any toxic substances.
- It's very important to make sure that your air fryer is standing on a flat, level surface whenever you want to use it. The air fryer should also have at least four inches of open space surrounding it so that the air fryer has enough space to safely expel excess heat and steam. If the air fryer is too crowded, it might overheat and break down. It's also important to keep any items that aren't heat resistant, such as plastic containers or paper, well away from the air fryer, as they may melt or combust. You should especially keep the outlets clear while the air fryer is in use.

POSSIBLE PROBLEMS AND SOLUTIONS

No matter how well you take care of your air fryer, it's still possible that you could come across some problems while working with your air fryer. Some problems may be serious, and you should always consult your user manual. Some problems may be very obvious or easy to deal with, while other problems are more difficult to track down and may need professional repairs. Here are some clear signs and potential solutions to some of the most common problems you may come across when working with your air fryer:

- A very common problem is trouble closing the air fryer, or the pan and basket getting stuck if you try to slide it into the air fryer. This is often one of two very simple problems. The first is that the basket may be too full, and you can solve this by removing some of the food and preparing your meal in batches. If that doesn't help, there is a good chance that the pan and basket aren't attached properly. Simply detach the two and try connecting them again. Make sure you hear a click, and you'll know the basket is slotted properly into the pan.
- Another common issue is that the air fryer has trouble turning on. This might be a big problem, or it might be a small one. The first thing you should do is check that the air fryer is plugged into the outlet properly, that the outlet is turned on, and that the outlet works properly. If the air fryer still doesn't work, look for any damage to the air fryer's electrical cables and wiring. If you find any damage, you should take your air fryer in for repairs. If you don't find any signs of damage, you should call a repair service or the manufacturer, as this might be a mechanical problem that you can't solve yourself.
- Sometimes the food in your air fryer may not be properly cooked, despite following the instructions on temperature and cooking time perfectly. This is most commonly the result of the air fryer being too full, which causes most of the heat to be absorbed by the top layer of food. Simply lessen the amount of food you cook at a time and prepare your meals in batches.
- Sometimes, even after cleaning your air fryer, there might still be a lingering smell of whatever you've been cooking. This is usually caused by foods with a very strong and pungent odor. A good way to prevent this is to make sure you clean your air fryer as soon as it's cooled down, rather than leaving it for later. If you do have a lingering smell, soak the pan and basket in soapy water for up to an hour and wash it again. If you still can't get rid of the smell after several washes, you can apply lemon juice to a paper towel or cloth and rub the juice over your air fryer. Leave the air fryer coated with lemon juice for half an hour and wash it again to get rid of the smell.
- Bubbling or peeling on the inside of your air fryer is a fairly common problem that you can't do much about. If the non-stick coating on your air fryer implements is scratched and damaged, or if the pan and basket aren't inserted into air fryer properly, the intense heat may cause the coating to

bubble and peel. The coating isn't toxic, and won't contaminate your food, but continued use may cause damage to your air fryer. There's no way to undo the damage, and you should check your warranty to see if you qualify for a replacement. You can also find replacement parts at specialized stores and online. Always make sure that the replacement parts match your air fryer model and brand.

- Smoke is also a sign of problems. White smoke is usually a result of excess grease left in the air fryer. The smoke won't cause any damage, and you simply need to turn off the air fryer and clean off the grease as soon as your air fryer is properly cooled down. Black smoke leaking out of your air fryer is a sign of serious internal problems. You should turn off the air fryer immediately, unplug it, and call a repair service or the manufacturer for assistance. Your air fryer will most likely need professional repairs or replacement.

2

ABOUT THE RECIPES

All the recipes in this book are specifically designed for the air fryer and have a simple layout. Each recipe will have a clear list of ingredients and straightforward, easy to understand instructions that will make following the recipe a breeze. The recipe will also have keywords and phrases before the ingredient list, such as fast, and family-based to act as a quick search tool and help you decide the most suitable recipe for every meal. The key phrases will quickly tell you about the most important elements of the recipe, such as general cooking time, ingredient types, and serving sizes.

- Fast: these recipes are quick and easy, and won't take more than fifteen to sixteen minutes to prepare.
- Long-term: these are recipes that require you to plan ahead. They will either have extremely long cooking times or have ingredients that will need to be marinated beforehand.
- Family-based: these are larger recipes that serve four or more people and are suitable for children.
- Bachelor: these recipes are fairly simple to prepare and have no more than two servings. Perfect for a single person looking to cook themselves a quick meal.
- Beginner: these are recipes that are very simple and easy, and especially suited to beginners.
- Vegetarian: these recipes don't contain any meat, but they do contain other animal-based products such as dairy and eggs.
- Vegan: these recipes contain purely plant-based products and no form of animal-based products whatsoever.

The recipes will also have a clear indication of both the cooking temperature and preset setting most suitable for the recipe. Most recipes will also have notes after the method with cooking tips, possible variations, and substitutions for ingredients that might be hard to come by. The recipes are also grouped together by type, making it even easier to find what you're looking for. The recipes will have a rough estimation of how long they will take and how many they will serve. Please keep in mind that these are estimations, and they can vary a little. The prep time before cooking can be altered by your level of experience, your ability to multitask, and whether or not you have someone helping you in the kitchen. The number of servings per recipe can also be slightly altered depending on the size of each serving.

These recipes are good guidelines to get you started, especially if you don't have that much cooking experience yet, but they aren't set in stone. I want to encourage you to play around and experiment with the recipes. Add some of your own ingredients and play around with your favorite spices. Take out ingredients you don't like and switch them out with something fairly similar that you do love to eat. If you've finished cooking and your food isn't quite as crispy as you'd like it, pop it back into the air fryer for another minute or two. (Just be careful not to leave it in too long, since you don't want to overcook and dry out your food.) If your food ends up being a little too crispy and well-done for your liking, make a note and reduce the cooking time a little bit next time. (Make sure that your food is still properly cooked and your meat still reaches a safe internal temperature to prevent any harmful bacteria.) Cooking - and eating - should be a joy, not a chore. Always try to prepare food that you and your whole family love to eat and enjoy the whole cooking process from start to finish.

3

BREAKFAST

Hard-Boiled Eggs

270°F
BAKE

PREP TIME: 1 MINUTE / COOKING TIME: 8 - 15 MINUTES
SERVES: 3 - 6

Boiled eggs are a classic addition to almost any breakfast, and are easy to prepare in the air fryer. There might be slight scorch marks where the eggs come into contact with the air fryer basket, but that is a minor flaw that won't affect the taste and quality in any way.

FAMILY-BASED, BEGINNER, VEGETARIAN

Ingredients:
6 eggs

Method:

1. Gently place the eggs in the air fryer basket in a single layer. Be careful not to damage the shells.
2. Bake the eggs to your liking. Use 8 minutes for a softer, more runny yolk, and 15 - 28 minutes for a harder yolk. Experiment a few times with your air fryer to find the perfect baking time that works for you.
3. Carefully remove the eggs using tongs, and submerge them in cold water to keep the eggs from cooking further inside the shells.
4. Let the eggs cool down in the water for at least five minutes. Peel the eggs and serve them as they are, or together with some toast or other breakfast treats.

Tips: This recipe is very easy to adapt and you can cook as many eggs as you want with this recipe, though it may be necessary to prepare them in batches. Hard-boiled eggs are also great for cooking in advance, as they will last two or three days if properly refrigerated. If you have trouble peeling the eggs, try peeling them underwater, as this might be a little easier.

Egg Muffins

PREP TIME: 7 MINUTES / COOKING TIME: 15 MINUTES / SERVES: 4

Egg muffins are an American classic, often also known as "quick breads" and are very easy to prepare. They should be served immediately, as they can become stale quite easily.

Method:
1. Mix the egg, milk, olive oil, Worcestershire sauce, baking powder, and flour together in a bowl and whisk well.
2. Divide the mixture into four muffin cups, sprinkle with parmesan, and arrange the cups in your air fryer basket. Bake for 15 minutes. Grease your muffin cups, especially if they're not silicon.
3. Carefully remove the muffin cups from the air fryer. Let cool slightly before removing the muffins from the cup.
4. Serve while still warm.

Tips: For a little added flavor, you can add some ingredients like chopped spinach, chopped onion, chopped tomato, and even some bacon bits if you want. It's advised to cook or fry these extra ingredients a little bit beforehand.

300°F BAKE

BEGINNER, FAMILY-BASED, VEGETARIAN

Ingredients:
- 1 egg
- 2 oz parmesan
- 3 tbsp milk
- 2 tbsp olive oil
- Worcestershire sauce to taste
- 1 tbsp baking powder
- 3.5 oz white flour

Sausage Breakfast Mix

300°F
BAKE

PREP TIME: 10 MINUTES / COOKING TIME: 30 MINUTES / SERVES: 6

This hearty breakfast can be served as is or with bread or toast. This recipe requires a pan or baking tray rather than a regular air fryer basket.

FAMILY-BASED

Ingredients:
- 1 ½ lbs smoked sausage, chopped & slightly browned
- 1 ½ cups grits
- 16 oz cheddar / gouda
- 4 ½ cups water
- 1 cup milk
- 4 eggs, whisked
- ¼ tsp garlic powder
- 1 ½ tsp thyme, chopped
- Salt and pepper to taste

Method:
1. Bring water to boil in a pot over medium heat. Stir in the grits, close with a lid, and let it cook for five minutes.
2. Remove the grits from the heat and stir in your shredded cheese. Keep stirring until the cheese melts fully, then whisk in the milk, eggs, garlic powder, thyme, salt, and pepper. Make sure everything is mixed very well.
3. Grease your pan or baking tray and place your browned sausage inside. Pour the grits mixture over the sausage and spread it evenly.
4. Cook for 25 minutes.
5. Transfer to a serving dish or divide the meal equally among the plates and serve immediately.

Tips: As a substitute, you can use polenta or cornmeal rather than grits, though your meal will have a smoother texture. If you don't have a pan or baking tray for your air fryer, you can use a metal bowl that fits neatly into your air fryer basket.

Strawberry and Cream Cheese French Toast Roll-Ups

PREP TIME: 15 MINUTES / COOKING TIME: 5 - 10 MINUTES
SERVES: 4 – 8

**300°F
BAKE**

This recipe brings the famous dessert "strawberries and cream" to a breakfast classic for a sweet, fruity twist.

**FAMILY-BASED,
VEGETARIAN**

Method:
1. Flatten the bread with a rolling pin and spread 1 tbsp of cream cheese over each slice. Spread the cream cheese in a strip, starting 1 inch from the edge of the bread.
2. Place 1 sliced strawberry on each strip of cream cheese, and roll the bread as tightly as possible.
3. Whisk the milk and eggs into a shallow bowl, making sure both ingredients are thoroughly mixed. Mix the sugar and cinnamon in another shallow bowl.
4. Coat each roll of bread first with the egg mixture and then with the sugar mixture, then spray lightly with a small amount of vegetable oil for that extra crisp.
5. Place the bread rolls in a single layer in your air fryer basket with the seam facing downward.
6. Cook in batches for 5 minutes per batch.
7. This dish can be served hot or cold.

Ingredients:
- 16 slices white bread, crusts removed
- 16 strawberries, thinly sliced
- 4 eggs
- 16 tbsp cream cheese, softened
- 6 tbsp milk
- 2/3 cup sugar
- 2 tsp cinnamon, ground

Tips: This dish can also be served as a dessert together with some cream, ice cream or chocolate sauce. You can also play around with this dish and experiment a little with different types of berries and other fruits. This recipe is also very easy to halve or double, as your batches will stay the same size, and there won't be a need to increase or decrease your cooking time.

Apple Pancakes

360°F
FRY

VEGAN,
BEGINNER,
FAMILY-BASED

PREP TIME: 10 MINUTES / COOKING TIME: 16 MINUTES / SERVES: 4

This recipe uses the best nature has to offer to bring you a healthy, sweet breakfast. This dish requires a pan or baking tray.

Ingredients:
- 1 cup apple, peeled, cored & diced
- 1 ¾ cups flour
- 2 tsp baking powder
- 2 tbsp sugar
- 1 cup almond milk
- ¼ tsp vanilla extract
- 1 tbsp flax seed, ground & mixed with 3 tbsp water
- 2 tsp cinnamon powder

Method:
1. Mix your flour, baking powder, sugar, vanilla extract, and cinnamon powder in a bowl. Mix well.
2. Add the apple, milk, and flax seed mixture while stirring. Stir until everything is well mixed and you don't have any lumps or clots.
3. Grease your pan or baking tray and spread ¼ of the batter onto the bottom.
4. Cook for 5 minutes per pancake, flipping the pancake over halfway through the cooking process.
5. Transfer the pancake onto the plate and cook the next pancake. Serve warm.

Tips: You can add all of your favorite pancakes to this dish if you like. To make this recipe suitable for type 2 diabetics, replace the flour with buckwheat or whole grain flour, and replace the sugar with fructose. When using fructose, use half the amount recommended by the recipe, as fructose is much sweeter than regular sugar.

26   Air Fryer Cookbook

Asparagus Frittata

PREP TIME: 10 MINUTES / COOKING TIME: 5 MINUTES / SERVES: 1 – 2

400°F
FRY

This egg-based Italian dish is very similar to omelets and scrambled eggs and is very easy to cook. Because this dish tastes amazing both warm and cold, it's great for a bachelor who wants a simple breakfast and can put the second serving away for lunch or a snack later in the day. This dish requires a pan or baking tray.

FAST, BEGINNER, BACHELOR, VEGETARIAN

Method:
1. Mix the eggs, parmesan, milk, salt, and pepper in a bowl. Whisk thoroughly.
2. Grease your pan or baking tray and fill with your asparagus. Pour the egg mixture over the asparagus tips and toss lightly.
3. Cook for 5 minutes.
4. Serve either warm or cold. The frittata can be served as is, or with bread.

Ingredients:
- 10 asparagus tips, steamed
- 4 eggs, whisked
- 2 tbsp parmesan, grated
- 4 tbsp milk
- Salt and pepper to taste

Tips: This dish is great for experimenting. You can switch the asparagus tips out with various other vegetables of your liking. You can even add ingredients like chopped sausages or tomatoes, and you aren't limited to a single ingredient. You can try adding some of your favorite herbs and spices. You can also garnish the dish with some extra shredded cheese and fresh tarragon.

Cheesy Breakfast Bread

350°F
TOAST

PREP TIME: 10 MINUTES / COOKING TIME: 8 MINUTES / SERVES: 3 - 6

This is a very simple and easy way to make tomato and cheese toast with a great twist and refined taste.

BEGINNER, VEGETARIAN

Method:
1. Lay out your bread slices on a flat, clean working surface. Spread butter over all your slices. Butter both sides if you want to add some extra crisp to your bread.
2. Spread each slice with 1 tsp of tomato pesto and top with garlic and mozzarella.
3. Place the bread in your air fryer basket in a single layer and cook for 8 minutes. It may be necessary to cook in batches.
4. Use tongs or a spatula to remove the bread without burning yourself, and serve while still hot.

Ingredients:
  6 bread slices
  1 cup mozzarella, grated
  3 garlic cloves, minced
  6 tsp sun-dried tomato pesto
  Butter or margarine

Tips: If you're looking for a somewhat different taste, you can switch out the tomato pesto with basil pesto or something similar.

Breakfast Doughnuts

PREP TIME: 10 MINUTES / COOKING TIME: 18 MINUTES /
SERVES: 3 - 6

This is a recipe for a classic dessert or coffee snack that has been adapted to suit the breakfast table and is a great treat for the whole family. Although a regular air fryer basket would suffice, this will work better with a pan.

Method:
1. Mix 2 tsp butter, egg yolks, and table sugar in a bowl and whisk together.
2. Stir in ¼ cup of sour cream. In a separate bowl, sift the flour and baking powder and mix well.
3. Add the flour mix and the rest of the sour cream to the egg mix. Stir well until you have a lump-free dough.
4. Roll the dough out on a floured surface and use cookie cutters to cut out your doughnuts.
5. Transfer your doughnuts to your pan or basket in a single layer and bake for 8 minutes. The doughnuts shouldn't touch each other and need enough space to rise properly while they bake. It may be necessary to bake the doughnuts in batches.
6. While the doughnuts are baking, mix the castor sugar and cinnamon powder thoroughly in a shallow bowl.
7. Use tongs to remove the doughnuts and dip them in the castor sugar mixture while they're still hot.
8. The doughnuts can be served hot or cold.

Did you know: The exact origin of the doughnut is uncertain, but the original shape was a stick of twisted dough. The doughnut became popular in the form of a ball in England and was often filled with jelly. The iconic ring shape of the doughnut was allegedly created by an American named Hansen Gregory in 1847 when he removed the center of an English doughnut because he didn't like the texture of that area.

360°F
BAKE

BEGINNER, VEGETARIAN, FAMILY-BASED

Ingredients:
- 2 tbsp butter, softened
- 2 egg yolks, beaten
- ½ cup sour cream
- 2 ¼ cups white flour
- 1 ½ tsp baking powder
- ½ cup sugar
- 1/3 cup castor sugar
- 1 tsp cinnamon powder

Spinach Parcels

400°F
BAKE

**FAST,
BACHELOR,
BEGINNER,
VEGETARIAN**

Ingredients:
    4 sheets filo pastry
    1 lb spinach/baby
        spinach, roughly
        chopped & stems
        removed
    2 tbsp pine nuts
    ½ lb ricotta cheese
    Zest from 1 lemon
    1 egg, whisked
    Salt and pepper to
    taste

This is a quick and simple breakfast recipe. A great advantage is that the filling can be made in large quantities and frozen for later use.

Method:
1. Mix the spinach, pine nuts, ricotta, lemon zest, egg, salt, and pepper in a bowl and stir well.
2. Lay out the sheets of pastry on a clean working surface and divide the spinach mix equally. Be careful to keep the mix in the middle of the pastry and away from the edges.
3. Fold each sheet of pastry diagonally to form the parcels and press the edges together firmly. Place the parcels in your basket and bake for 4 minutes.
4. Use tongs to remove the parcels and serve them while still hot. The spinach parcels can also be served together with greek yogurt.

Tips: This is another good recipe to adapt for larger quantities and to experiment with. You can add some chopped, browned onions instead of the pine nuts for a different taste. You can also experiment with different cheeses that can be combined with the ricotta cheese or can replace it completely.

Espresso Oatmeal

PREP TIME: 6 MINUTES / COOKING TIME: 17 MINUTES / SERVES: 4

360°F
BAKE

This recipe takes a breakfast classic and combines it with another common breakfast tradition, namely coffee. This recipe requires a deep pan or baking tray.

BEGINNER, VEGETARIAN

Method:
1. Mix the oats, sugar, espresso powder, milk, and water in your pan or baking tray and stir well.
2. Cook for 17 minutes.
3. Remove the pan from your air fryer and stir in the vanilla extract. Let the oats cool down for 5 minutes.
4. Serve while still warm.

Ingredients:
- 1 cup steel cut oats
- 2 tbsp sugar
- 1 tsp espresso powder
- 1 cup milk
- 2 ½ cups water
- 2 tsp vanilla extract

Tips: This is another recipe that is easy to adapt for larger or smaller quantities. You can also increase and decrease the amount of espresso powder and sugar according to taste.

Greek Potato Mix

PREP TIME: 10 MINUTES / COOKING TIME: 20 MINUTES / SERVES: 4

This is a healthy, hearty breakfast that is easy to prepare and that your whole family is bound to enjoy.

**LONG-TERM,
BEGINNER,
VEGAN,
FAMILY-BASED**

Ingredients:
  1 ½ lbs potatoes,
    peeled, cubed
  3 ½ oz coconut
    cream
  2 tbsp olive oil
  1 tbsp paprika
  Salt and pepper to
  taste

Method:
  1. Submerge the cubed potatoes in water and let them soak for 10 - 30 minutes to remove all excess starch. Drain the potatoes and pat them dry.
  2. Mix 1 tbsp olive oil with the paprika, salt, and pepper in a bowl, and toss your potato cubes in the mixture. Make sure the potatoes are properly coated.
  3. Place the potatoes in your basket and bake for 20 minutes.
  4. Mix the coconut cream and the rest of the olive oil in a bowl and add salt and pepper to taste. Mix thoroughly.
  5. Serve the potato mix while still warm, with a dollop of the coconut cream mixture on top.

Tips: If you like the additional flavor and texture, you can leave the peels on the potatoes. You can also switch the regular paprika out for hot paprika and add some garlic for extra taste. You can add a bit of lemon or lime juice to the olive oil coating for a more zesty taste to your potato mix.

4

SNACKS & APPETIZERS

Spring Rolls

360°F
BAKE

PREP TIME: 10 MINUTES / COOKING TIME: 28 MINUTES / SERVES: 8

This is a classic appetizer that works great for every opportunity.

VEGETARIAN, BEGINNER, FAMILY-BASED

Ingredients:
- 10 spring roll sheets
- 2 cups cabbage, shredded
- 2 medium onions, finely chopped
- 1 carrot, grated
- 2 tbsp fresh ginger, grated
- 3 cloves garlic, minced
- ½ chili pepper, seeded & minced
- 2 tbsp olive oil
- 2 tbsp water
- 1 tsp soy sauce
- 1 tsp sugar
- 2 tbsp corn flour
- Salt and pepper to taste

Method:
1. Heat the olive oil in a pan over medium heat and fry the onions until slightly browned. Add the cabbage, carrot, ginger, garlic, chili pepper, soy sauce, sugar, salt, and pepper, stirring well.
2. Cook the filling for 2 - 3 minutes and remove from the heat. Let the filling cool down for a few minutes.
3. Cut the spring roll sheets into squares of your preferred size. Divide the cabbage filling equally between all your spring roll sheets, making sure to stay clear of the edges, and roll the sheets.
4. Mix the flour and water in a bowl, stirring well, and dip the spring rolls in the mixture. make sure the spring rolls are fully coated.
5. Place the spring rolls in your air fryer basket in a single layer and cook them for 20 minutes, flipping your spring rolls halfway through the baking process. It may be necessary to cook the spring rolls in batches.
6. Use tongs to remove the spring rolls. Serve them while hot, with a suitable dipping sauce if you want.

Tips: When working with fresh garlic, use the flat of your knife blade to crush each clove before mincing. This will bring out more flavor and will start a chemical reaction within the garlic that can help with cancer prevention.

Cajun Shrimp Appetizer

PREP TIME: 10 MINUTES / COOKING TIME: 5 MINUTES / SERVES: 2

**390°F
FRY**

This is a very simple and easy appetizer that is great for times when you're in a hurry.

Method:
1. Mix the oil, seasoning, paprika, salt, and pepper in a bowl and mix well. Toss the shrimp in the mix and make sure they're coated thoroughly.
2. Place the shrimp in your air fryer basket and cook for 5 minutes.
3. Use tongs to remove the shrimp and serve on a platter.

Tips: If you're having trouble getting your hands on old bay seasoning, there are several recipes available on how to make your own. You can also spend some time experimenting with different types of seafood seasonings.

FAST, BACHELOR, BEGINNER

Ingredients:
  20 tiger shrimp, deveined & peeled
  1 tbsp olive oil
  ½ tsp old bay seasoning
  ¼ tsp smoked paprika
  Salt and pepper to taste

Sweet Popcorn

400°F
BAKE

FAST,
BEGINNER,
VEGETARIAN,
FAMILY-BASED

Ingredients:
- 2 tbsp popcorn kernels
- 2 oz brown sugar
- 2 ½ tbsp butter

PREP TIME: 5 MINUTES / COOKING TIME: 10 MINUTES / SERVES: 4

This is a sweet treat that the whole family can enjoy together. This recipe requires a pan or baking tray.

Method:
1. Cook your kernels for 6 minutes in your air fryer. Transfer your popcorn onto a clean tray once done and set aside.
2. Melt the butter in a frying pan over low heat. Add the sugar to the butter and stir until all the sugar is dissolved.
3. Add the popcorn to the syrup and toss, coating the popcorn. Move the popcorn back to the tray and drizzle the remaining syrup over the popcorn. Let it cool down.
4. Serve as a snack once the syrup has cooled down completely.

Tips: For this recipe, you can experiment with adding extra flavors to the syrup, such as vanilla, almond, or caramel extract.

Stuffed Peppers

400°F
FRY

This is another classic appetizer that's always a hit and can easily be adapted for larger or smaller portions.

VEGETARIAN,
BEGINNER

Method:
1. Mix the cheese, oil, salt, and pepper in a bowl. Toss the cheese to make sure each piece is thoroughly coated.
2. Stuff the peppers with the cheese, and divide the remaining oil mixture between the peppers.
3. Place the peppers in your air fryer basket and cook for 8 minutes.
4. Use tongs to remove the peppers and serve while hot.

Ingredients:
   8 small bell peppers, tops removed, seeded
   3.5 oz goat cheese, divided into 8 pieces
   1 tbsp olive oil
   Salt and pepper to taste

Tips: This dish has a lot of space for experimenting. There are lots of cheeses, such as feta, blue cheese, ricotta, etc. that will make an excellent substitute for the goat cheese. You can also add ingredients to your stuffing, such as finely chopped onion or chili pepper for an extra twist.

Honey Party Wings

360°F
FRY

PREP TIME: 1 HOUR, 10 MINUTES / COOKING TIME: 12 MINUTES / SERVES: 8

LONG-TERM,
BEGINNER,
FAMILY-BASED

This is a simple and easy dish that has a lovely sweet and sour flavor. This makes a great appetizer, but can also be served as finger food at any event.

Ingredients:
   16 chicken wings,
      halved
   2 tbsp honey
   2 tbsp soy sauce
   2 tbsp lime juice
   Salt and pepper to
   taste

Method:
1. Mix the honey, soy sauce, lime juice, salt, and pepper together in a bowl. Toss the chicken wings in the marinade and let rest for 1 hour in the refrigerator.
2. Pat the chicken wings dry and place them in your air fryer basket in a single layer.
3. Cook for 12 minutes. Make sure to flip the wings halfway through. It may be necessary to cook in batches.
4. The chicken wings can be served hot or cold.

Tips: If you don't have any lime juice, lemon juice will make an excellent substitute. You can stir a tsp mustard into the marinade for a honey mustard chicken wing, or you can add fresh, chopped herbs for a little extra flavor.

Eggplant Appetizer Salad

PREP TIME: 10 MINUTES / COOKING TIME: 20 MINUTES / SERVES: 4

370°F
BAKE

This is a fresh, healthy appetizer that can easily be adapted for larger or smaller quantities. The size of the serving can also be adapted to make a light meal rather than just an appetizer. This recipe requires a pan or baking tray.

BEGINNER,
VEGAN,
FAMILY-BASED

Method:
1. Mix the oregano, vinegar, salt, and pepper in your pan. Toss the eggplant, tomato, and olives in the vinegar to coat everything.
2. Cook for 20 minutes, shaking regularly.
3. Garnish with fresh oregano and serve while still hot.

Ingredients:
  3 cups eggplant, cubed
  1 ½ cups tomatoes, roughly chopped
  6 oz black olives, pitted & sliced
  1 tbsp oregano, chopped
  2 tsp balsamic vinegar
  Salt and pepper to taste

Tips: If your recipe specifies dried herbs and you prefer to use fresh herbs, use twice the amount of herbs specified to achieve the same amount of flavor.

Crispy Radish Chips

350°F
BAKE

PREP TIME: 10 MINUTES / COOKING TIME: 10 MINUTES / SERVES: 4

BEGINNER,
VEGAN,
FAMILY-BASED

This is a healthier alternative to potato chips and is a great snack for the whole family. This recipe can be applied to potatoes if you want the original potato chip.

Ingredients:
- 15 radishes, thinly sliced
- 1 tbsp chives, finely chopped
- Cooking oil
- Salt and pepper to taste

Method:
1. Lay the radish slices on a clean tray. Very lightly drizzle or spray the radishes with cooking oil on both sides. Season with salt and pepper.
2. Transfer your radish slices to your air fryer basket and bake for 10 minutes. Shake or flip halfway through. For the best results, work with only a single layer of slices. This may require baking the chips in batches.
3. Sprinkle the chives over the chips and serve.

Did you know: The earliest recipes similar to potato chips date back as far as 1817 in England, but a popular legend claims that potato chips as we know them today were created by accident in 1853 by George Crum, who sliced potatoes extremely thin, fried them to a crisp and added large amounts of salt when a customer complained that his french fries were too thick, soggy, and under-seasoned.

Sweet Bacon Snack

PREP TIME: 10 MINUTES / COOKING TIME: 30 MINUTES / SERVES: 4 – 16

300°F
BAKE

This may seem like an odd combination, but this meaty snack is sure to be a hit with both kids and adults.

BEGINNER,
FAMILY-BASED

Method:
1. Place the bacon slices in a single layer in your air fryer basket and sprinkle with cinnamon powder. Cook for 30 minutes.
2. While the bacon is cooking, heat the avocado oil in a frying pan over medium heat. Stir in the chocolate until it's completely melted. You can grate or chop the chocolate to let it melt faster.
3. Stir in the maple extract and remove from heat. Let the chocolate cool for a while. Once the bacon is done cooking, use tongs to remove the slices and let them cool down.
4. Dip the bacon slices in the chocolate and lay them out on parchment paper.
5. Let the bacon cool completely before serving.

Ingredients:
    16 bacon slices
    3 oz dark chocolate
    1 tbsp avocado oil
    1 tsp maple extract
    ½ tsp cinnamon
       powder

Tips: If you want a slightly less sweet taste, use dark chocolate with a 60 – 70% cocoa content. You can also experiment with the chocolate mixture by adding some vanilla extract or more cinnamon powder.

Cheese Sticks

390°F
FRY

BEGINNER,
LONG-TERM,
VEGETARIAN,
FAMILY-BASED

Ingredients:
  8 mozzarella
    cheese strings,
    halved
  1 cup parmesan,
    grated
  1 clove garlic,
    minced
  2 eggs, whisked
  Cooking oil
  1 tbsp Italian
    seasoning
  Salt and pepper to
    taste

PREP TIME: 1 HOUR, 10 MINUTES / COOKING TIME: 8 MINUTES / SERVES: 4 - 16

Although frozen cheese sticks are easy to buy in a store, you may not have the time or opportunity to go out to buy them. Freshly made cheese sticks are simple, easy, and use fairly common ingredients you are likely to have at home.

Method:
  1. Mix the parmesan, garlic, seasoning, salt, and pepper in a bowl to create a crumb-like coating. Mix thoroughly.
  2. Dip each mozzarella cheese string in the whisked eggs, and then in the parmesan coating. Make sure the mozzarella is coated properly. Add a second layer of whisked egg and parmesan coating.
  3. Keep the cheese sticks frozen for at least 1 hour.
  4. Remove any excess ice that may have formed, and lightly drizzle or spray the cheese sticks with cooking oil.
  5. Place the cheese sticks in your air fryer basket in a single layer and cook for 8 minutes. Flip the cheese sticks halfway. You may need to cook the cheese sticks in batches.
  6. Use tongs to remove the cheese sticks. Serve hot with dipping sauces.

Tips: If you don't have mozzarella cheese strings, simply cut regular mozzarella cheese into rectangles in a size to your liking. You can also experiment with the seasoning in your cheese coating, such as adding paprika, chili powder, or other spices and seasonings you like.

Mini Beef Pie

PREP TIME: 1 HOUR, 20 MINUTES / COOKING TIME: 34 MINUTES / SERVES: 12

370°F
BAKE

Flaky dough filled with ground beef. A great starter for large events. This recipe requires muffin trays that will fit in your air fryer.

BEGINNER,
LONG-TERM,
FAMILY-BASED

Method:
1. Mix the butter, water, vinegar, 4 cups flour and ½ tbsp salt in a bowl. Knead gently until you have a dough. Flatten the dough, wrap it with plastic, and keep refrigerated for 1 hour.
2. While the dough rests, fry the ground beef in the oil in a frying pan over medium heat. Add the carrots, leeks, and garlic and cook for 4 minutes. Add the tomato paste, 1 tbsp flour and curry paste, and fry briefly. Add the coconut milk and cook for 1o minutes. Take off the heat, season with salt and pepper, and let cool.
3. Roll the dough out on a floured work surface. Use a cookie cutter to cut out 12 circles roughly 5 inches in diameter, and 12 circles roughly 2 inches in diameter. Grease your muffin trays thoroughly and place a large circle of dough in each cup. Prick the bottom of each circle with a fork.
4. Divide the filling between the cups and cover with the smaller circles. Press the edges together with a fork and lightly score the lid and brush with the egg. Cook for 24 minutes. It may be necessary to cook the pies in batches. Remove the pies from the tray and let cool slightly.
5. Stir the sour cream and coriander together and serve with the pies.

Ingredients:
- 1 lb ground beef
- ½ lb carrots, chopped
- ½ lb leeks, chopped
- 1 clove garlic, minced
- ½ lb butter, cold & cut into pieces
- 1 egg, whisked
- 1 tbsp oil
- 2 tbsp tomato paste
- ½ cup sour cream
- ¾ cup coconut milk
- ¾ cup ice cold water
- 1 tbsp cider vinegar
- 4 cups & 1 tbsp flour
- 2 tbsp curry powder
- 8 stems coriander, chopped
- Salt and pepper to taste

Tips: For an alternate taste, you can leave out the curry powder and use port, red wine, or rosemary for flavor. You can also add red pepper flakes or chopped chili pepper for some extra heat.

5

SEAFOOD DISHES

Soy Salmon Steaks

330°F
BAKE

PREP TIME: 2 HOURS, 10 MINUTES / COOKING TIME: 8 MINUTES / SERVES: 2

LONG-TERM,
BEGINNER

Ingredients:
  2 salmon fillets
  1/3 cup brown
    sugar
  2 tbsp olive oil
  1/3 cup light soy
    sauce
  1/3 cup water
  Juice from 1 large
    lemon
  1/8 tsp garlic
    powder
  Salt and pepper to
  taste

Despite its long marinating time, this dish is very easy to prepare and is great for beginners. It's filled with soft and delicate flavors.

Method:
1. Mix the sugar, olive oil, soy sauce, water, and lemon juice in a bowl. Stir well.
2. If your salmon was recently frozen, pat your fillets dry with paper towels to remove any excess moisture. Season the fillets with garlic powder, salt, and pepper. Put the salmon fillets in the marinade and make sure they're covered fully. Cover the bowl and let the fish marinate in the refrigerator for 2 hours.
3. Once the salmon is done marinating, lightly pat dry with paper towels to remove excess marinade. Place the fillets in your air fryer basket and cook for 8 minutes. If your fillets are very thick, you may need to cook them a little longer.
4. Garnish with some fresh parsley if you want, and serve with rice or salad.

Did you know: Although dark and light soy sauce are made in almost the exact same way, dark soy sauce is generally thicker and has an added sweetness from sources like molasses or sugar, while light soy sauce is a bit thinner and saltier. The type of soy sauce you use can have a large impact on the taste and texture of your food.

Tuna and Chimichurri Sauce

360°F
BAKE

This Argentinian inspired dish is great for a slightly lighter meal and is ideal for those who love spicy foods.

BEGINNER

Method:
1. Chimichurri Sauce. Mix the onion, jalapeno pepper, garlic, vinegar, ⅓ cup olive oil, cilantro, parsley, basil, and thyme in a bowl. Make sure the vinegar and oil are well mixed.
2. Season your tuna steak with salt and pepper, and rub thoroughly with the remaining 2 tbsp olive oil.
3. Place the steak in your air fryer basket and cook for 6 minutes, turning the steak halfway through.
4. Toss the arugula in the chimichurri sauce you've prepared and divide among the servings.
5. Cut and divide the tuna steak and plate together with the arugula. Pour the rest of the chimichurri sauce over the tuna and serve.

Tips: To make this meal more family-friendly, you can simply leave out the jalapeno pepper and red pepper flakes. If you are making food for both people who like spicy food and people who don't, complete the sauce without the jalapeno and red pepper flakes. Divide the sauce into two separate bowls and add half the specified amount of jalapeno and red pepper flakes to one bowl.

Ingredients:
- 1 lb sushi tuna steak
- 6 oz baby arugula
- 1 small red onion, finely chopped
- 1 jalapeno pepper, finely chopped
- 2 avocados, peeled & sliced
- 3 cloves garlic, minced
- 3 tbsp balsamic vinegar
- 1/3 cup + 2 tbsp olive oil
- ½ cup cilantro, chopped
- 2 tbsp parsley, chopped
- 2 tbsp basil, chopped
- 1 tsp thyme, chopped
- 1 tsp red pepper flakes
- Salt and pepper to taste

Garlic Ginger Shrimp

350°F
BAKE

PREP TIME: 1 HOUR, 15 MINUTES / COOKING TIME: 8 MINUTES / SERVES: 1 - 3

BEGINNER,
BACHELOR,
LONG-TERM

This is a very easy to prepare dish that is made more convenient by the fact that the marinade can be made a day or two ahead of time.

Ingredients:
- 1 lb shrimp, deveined and peeled
- 2 green onions, finely chopped
- 2 cloves garlic, chopped
- 1 tsp ginger, grated
- 1 ½ tsp sugar
- 3 tbsp butter
- 2 tsp lime juice, freshly squeezed
- Cooking oil

Method:
1. Bring the onions, garlic, ginger, sugar, butter, and lime juice to a simmer in a saucepan over low heat. Remove from heat before it boils and let the marinade cool down.
2. Place the shrimp in the marinade and make sure each shrimp is properly coated. Cover the bowl and let the shrimp marinate for at least an hour in the refrigerator. It's safe to let the shrimp marinate overnight.
3. Once the shrimp is done marinating, gently pat dry with paper towels to remove excess marinade. Drizzle or spray lightly with cooking oil and place in the air fryer basket.
4. Cook for 8 minutes, turning the shrimp halfway through. If the shrimp are very large, you may need to extend the cooking time a little.
5. Use tongs to remove the shrimp. The shrimp can be served as is, with other side dishes, or as part of a seafood platter.

Tips: If you plan to make this dish more than once within a short period of time, you can make larger quantities of the marinade in one go. Keep the marinade in a large, sealable container and pour some into a smaller bowl to marinate the shrimp. Keep the rest of the marinade refrigerated, and it should last for a few days. Once you're done marinating the shrimp, discard the used marinade. Do not return it to the container with the rest of the marinade.

Asian Salmon

PREP TIME: 1 HOUR, 5 MINUTES / COOKING TIME: 15 MINUTES / SERVES: 2

A lovely salmon with a traditional Asian marinade.

Method:
1. Mix the honey, soy sauce, mirin, and water in a bowl. Whisk together thoroughly.
2. Put the salmon in the bowl and rub with the marinade. Let rest in the refrigerator for at least 1 hour.
3. Place the salmon in the air fryer basket after marinating and cook for 15 minutes. Flip the fillets after the first 7 minutes.
4. Pour the marinade in a saucepan while the salmon is cooking and bring to a boil over medium heat. Whisk well while heating. Cook the marinade for 2 - 3 minutes and take off the heat.
5. Drizzle the marinade over the salmon fillets when serving.

Tips: Mirin is a sweet Japanese rice wine that can be difficult to get your hands on sometimes, but you can use more common ingredients to make a usable substitute. Mix 1 - 2 tbsp of sugar and ½ cup of white wine, dry sherry, or vermont to substitute ½ cup mirin.

360°F
BAKE

BEGINNER,
BACHELOR,
LONG-TERM

Ingredients:
- 2 salmon fillets, medium-sized
- 6 tbsp honey
- 6 tbsp light soy sauce
- 3 tsp mirin
- 1 tsp water

Swordfish with Mango Salsa

FAST,
BEGINNER,
BACHELOR

Ingredients:
- 2 swordfish steaks, medium-sized
- 1 mango, chopped
- 1 orange, peeled & sliced
- 1 avocado, peeled & chopped
- 2 tsp avocado oil
- ½ tbsp balsamic vinegar
- 1 tbsp cilantro, chopped
- Pinch of garlic powder
- Pinch of onion powder
- Pinch of cumin
- Salt and pepper to taste

PREP TIME: 8 MINUTES / COOKING TIME: 6 MINUTES / SERVES: 1 - 2

This fish may be expensive, but it goes great with the tropical taste of mango salsa, and this is a good dish to make for a romantic date.

Method:
1. Season the swordfish with the onion powder, garlic powder, cumin, salt, and pepper, and rub with 1 tsp avocado oil.
2. Place the fillets in your air fryer basket and cook for 6 minutes. Flip the fillets halfway.
3. While the fish is cooking, mix the mango, avocado, remaining avocado oil, balsamic vinegar, cilantro, salt, and pepper in a bowl. Stir well to create the salsa.
4. Serve the fillets, topped with the salsa and the orange slices to the side.

Tips: As swordfish is expensive and often difficult to get your hands on, you can substitute it with any white fish that is very meaty. Good examples of swordfish substitutes are tuna, halibut, marlin, and shark.

Buttered Shrimp Skewers

PREP TIME: 10 MINUTES / COOKING TIME: 6 MINUTES / SERVES: 2 – 4

360°F
BAKE

This is a rich and flavorful, yet simple and easy dish that is served in a fun way.

FAST,
BEGINNER,
BACHELOR

Method:
1. Mix the garlic, butter, rosemary, salt, and pepper in a bowl and toss the shrimp and pepper slices in the mix. Make sure the shrimp and bell pepper are properly coated and let rest for 10 minutes.
2. Pat dry with paper towels to remove excess marinade and skewer the shrimp and bell pepper by alternating 2 shrimp and two slices of bell pepper per skewer. Place the skewers in your air fryer basket and cook for six minutes.
3. Use tongs to remove the skewers and serve while still hot.

Ingredients:
- 8 shrimp, deveined and peeled
- 8 slices green bell pepper
- 4 cloves garlic, minced
- 1 tbsp butter, melted
- 1 tbsp rosemary, chopped
- Salt and pepper to taste

Tips: This recipe is very easy to adapt for larger quantities and can work with tiger shrimp as well. As an alternative to skewering, you can cook the shrimp and bell pepper slices loosely and serve as they are. You can also cook the marinade over medium heat for two minutes and serve as a sauce with the shrimp and bell pepper over pasta. This works especially well with baby shrimp, but you will need to adapt your cooking time.

Cod Fillets with Fennel & Grape Salad

**400°F
ROAST**

BEGINNER,
BACHELOR

Ingredients:
- 2 cod fillets, deboned
- 1 bulb fennel, thinly sliced
- 1 cup grapes, halved
- ½ cup pecans
- 1 tbsp olive oil
- Salt and pepper to taste

PREP TIME: 10 MINUTES / COOKING TIME: 15 MINUTES / SERVES: 2

This is a fresh, simple salad that will work great as a light meal as well as in smaller servings. This dish requires a pan or a baking tray.

Method:
1. Lightly drizzle the fillets with ½ tbsp olive oil and season with salt and pepper. Rub the seasoning thoroughly into the fish.
2. Place the cod fillets in your air fryer basket and cook for 10 minutes.
3. Meanwhile, mix the fennel, grapes, pecans, remaining olive oil, salt, and pepper in a bowl and stir well. Make sure the fennel and grapes are properly coated.
4. Transfer the mix to a pan or baking tray, and cook for 5 minutes once the cod is done.
5. Plate the cod and drizzle the fennel mix over the cod and to the side, and serve immediately.

Tips: Although any type of cod will suffice, the best type to use is black cod, also known as "sablefish". You can play around with different types of nuts for new flavors, and for an extra burst of freshness and crispness, you can add some fresh fennel and grapes when serving.

Homemade Calamari Rings

PREP TIME: 5 MINUTES / COOKING TIME: 8 MINUTES / SERVES: 1 - 2

This recipe is much healthier than calamari rings bought at a restaurant and adds that extra freshness from being homemade, rather than just frozen calamari rings heated up.

Method:
1. Blend the oats in a food processor until fine. Mix with the parsley and paprika in a shallow bowl.
2. Season the calamari with salt and pepper and drizzle with lemon juice.
3. Dip the calamari in the oats mix, making sure everything is coated properly. Dip the calamari in the whisked egg and then in the oats a second time.
4. Place the calamari rings in your air fryer basket and cook for 8 minutes.
5. Use tongs to remove the calamari rings and serve while still warm.

Tips: For an alternate taste and texture, you can substitute the oats with dried bread crumbs or cornflake crumbs. Calamari can easily become tough and chewy if it isn't thoroughly cooked, so make sure that your calamari rings aren't too thick.

360°F
BAKE

BEGINNER,
FAST,
BACHELOR

Ingredients:
  1 oz calamari, sliced into thin rings
  1 cup oats
  Juice from 1 small lemon
  1 egg, whisked
  1 tsp parsley
  1 tbsp paprika
  Salt and pepper to taste

Parmesan Crumbed Fish

370°F BAKE

FAST,
BEGINNER,
BACHELOR

Ingredients:
- 2 cod fillets
- 1 clove garlic, minced
- ⅓ cup parmesan, finely grated
- 2 tsp dijon mustard
- 1 tbsp olive oil
- ½ cup panko bread crumbs
- Salt and pepper to taste

PREP TIME: 5 MINUTES / COOKING TIME: 5 MINUTES / SERVES: 2

A very quick and simple recipe for perfectly cooked fish with a crunchy parmesan coating on top. This dish requires a pan.

Method:
1. Season the fish with salt and pepper, and spread the dijon mustard on only one side.
2. Mix the garlic, parmesan, olive oil, bread crumbs, and a pinch of salt together in a shallow bowl. Press the mustard side of the fish into the crumb mix. Place the fish on your pan with the crumbed side facing upward and cook for 5 minutes. If the fillets are an inch or more thick, you may need to extend the cooking time.
3. Serve immediately.

Tips: This recipe works well with any type of firm white fish, such as tilapia, haddock, bass, and catfish. For additional taste, you can add some chopped parsley to the crumb mix.

6

MEAT DISHES

Pork Chops and Roasted Peppers

PREP TIME: 10 MINUTES / COOKING TIME: 16 MINUTES / SERVES: 4

A simple - and easy to make - meal for the whole family. This dish requires a pan or baking tray.

BEGINNER, FAMILY-BASED

Ingredients:
- 4 pork chops
- 2 bell peppers, sliced
- 3 cloves garlic, chopped
- 3 tbsp olive oil
- 3 tbsp lemon juice
- 2 tbsp thyme, chopped
- 1 tbsp smoked paprika
- Salt and pepper to taste

Method
1. Place the peppers in the pan and roast for a few minutes until slightly charred.
2. Chop the peppers and mix in your pan with the garlic, oil, lemon juice, thyme, paprika, salt, and pepper. Stir well.
3. Add the pork chops and make sure they're coated properly. Cook for 16 minutes.
4. Plate the pork chops and drizzle with the sauce and peppers.

Tips: This recipe works best with pork chops with the bone in but will still be fine with deboned pork chops. The sauce will also work great over rice.

Filet Mignon with Mushroom Sauce

PREP TIME: 10 MINUTES / COOKING TIME: 25 MINUTES / SERVES: 4

360°F
BAKE

A tender cut of beef, with a rich, creamy mushroom sauce.

FAMILY-BASED

Method:
1. Fry the shallot and garlic in olive oil in a frying pan over medium heat. Cook for 3 minutes, stirring occasionally. Stir in the mushrooms and cook further for 4 minutes.
2. Stir in the wine and cook until the wine has evaporated. Stir in the coconut cream, mustard, parsley, salt, and pepper. Cook for another 6 minutes and remove from heat.
3. Season the fillets with salt and pepper and place in your air fryer basket. Cook for 10 minutes. If your steaks are very thick, you may need to extend your cooking time.
4. Plate the fillets together with the sauce and serve.

Ingredients:
   4 fillet mignons
   12 mushrooms, sliced
   1 shallot, chopped
   2 cloves garlic, chopped
   1 ¼ cups coconut cream
   ¼ cup Dijon mustard
   2 tbsp olive oil
   ¼ cup wine
   2 tbsp parsley, chopped
   Salt and pepper to taste

Did you know: Filet mignon is a specific cut of beef tenderloin, but in French cooking, this cut is called filet de boeuf, and the term "filet mignon" refers to a cut of pork sirloin.

Mediterranean Steak and Scallops

360°F
BAKE

A tropical, exotic surf and turf dish bound to tickle your taste buds. This dish requires a pan or baking tray.

BEGINNER

Ingredients:
- 2 beef steaks
- 10 sea scallops
- 1 shallot, chopped
- 4 cloves garlic, minced
- ¼ cup butter
- 1 tsp lemon zest
- 2 tbsp lemon juice
- ¼ cup vegetable stock
- 2 tbsp basil, chopped
- 2 tbsp parsley, chopped
- Salt and pepper to taste

Method:
1. Season the steaks with salt and pepper, and place them in your air fryer basket. Cook for 10 minutes. Move the steaks to your pan or baking tray once done.
2. Add the scallops, shallot, garlic, butter, lemon zest and juice, vegetable stock, basil, and parsley. Toss lightly to make sure the steaks and scallops are properly coated, and cook for another 4 minutes.
3. Plate the scallops and steaks and drizzle the sauce over them. Serve while still warm.

Tips: If the beef turns out over or under-cooked compared to your liking, make a note, and shorten or extend the initial cooking time of the beef next time you prepare the dish. You can also experiment with additional herbs.

Crispy Asian Dumplings

A simple, yet delicious Asian classic that can act as a full meal, finger food, or part of a platter.

BEGINNER, FAMILY-BASED

Method:
1. After cooking the ground pork, mix with the cabbage, onion, chestnuts, ginger, soy sauce, and sesame oil in a bowl to make the filling.
2. Lay the wonton wrappers out on a flat surface, and place a piled tbsp of filling in the middle of each wrapper. Use your fingertips to moisten the edges of the wonton wrappers before folding the wrapper in half. Pinch the edges together to seal the dumpling.
3. Spray or drizzle the dumplings lightly with cooking oil and place in your air fryer basket in a single layer. Cook for 10 minutes, and turn the dumplings over halfway. You will most likely need to cook the dumplings in batches.
4. Serve the hot dumplings together with dipping sauces.

Ingredients:
- 1 lb ground pork, cooked to your preference and crumbed
- 4 cups cabbage, shredded
- 24 wonton wrappers
- 1 tbsp green onion, finely chopped
- ¼ cup chestnuts, chopped
- ½ tbsp fresh ginger, grated
- 1 tbsp soy sauce
- 1 tsp sesame oil
- Cooking oil

Tips: Although wonton wrappers are fairly easy to come by, you can make your own using flour, water, and eggs. With this recipe, you can explore a little by changing the meat in the filling, such as ground beef or turkey, or shredded chicken. You can also add more flavor by using herbs and spices while cooking your meat.

Beef Kabobs

370°F
BAKE

PREP TIME: 10 MINUTES / COOKING TIME: 10 MINUTES / SERVES: 2 - 4

BEGINNER,
FAMILY-BASED

This dish is simple and easy, and is great for social events. This recipe is also very easy to adapt for larger quantities.

Ingredients:
- 2 lb sirloin steak, cut into medium-sized cubes
- 2 red bell peppers, roughly chopped
- 1 zucchini, sliced
- 1 red onion, roughly chopped
- Juice from 1 lime, freshly squeezed
- ¼ cup olive oil
- ¼ cup salsa
- ½ tbsp cumin, ground
- 2 tbsp chili powder (optional)
- 2 tbsp hot sauce (optional)
- Salt and pepper to taste

Method:
1. Mix the lime juice, oil, salsa, cumin, salt, and pepper in a bowl and stir thoroughly. You can add the chili powder and hot sauce if you want your kabobs to be spicy.
2. Alternate your beef, bell pepper, zucchini, and onion on skewers until all your ingredients are used up. Use a brush to cover your skewers with the salsa you made.
3. Place the skewers in your air fryer basket in a single row and cook for 10 minutes. Turn your kabobs over halfway. You may need to cook your kabobs in batches.
4. Serve the kabobs together with a fresh salad.

Tips: There are various different types of salsa available to buy, from which you can choose your favorite for this recipe. You can also make your own salsa to add to this salsa mix. For a dash of extra color, you can use one red bell pepper and one yellow bell pepper, rather than just two red bell peppers.

Lamb and Green Pesto

PREP TIME: 1 HOUR / COOKING TIME: 45 MINUTES / SERVES: 4

300°F
ROAST

Although this meal takes some time to prepare, it's very simple and straightforward, and it has a very refined taste. This recipe requires a baking dish that will fit in your air fryer.

LONG-TERM, BEGINNER, FAMILY-BASED

Method
1. Mix the onion, lemon zest, pistachios, oil, mint, parsley, salt, and pepper in a food processor and blend until the ingredients form a paste.
2. Rub the lamb thoroughly with the pesto, and place in a covered bowl. Let the lamb rest for at least 1 hour in the refrigerator.
3. Place the lamb in your baking dish and drizzle with the lemon juice. Add the garlic and cook for 45 minutes.
4. Use tongs to remove the riblets and serve with your favorite sides.

Ingredients:
 2 lbs lamb riblets
 ½ onion, chopped
 1 small yellow onion, roughly chopped
 5 cloves garlic
 1 tsp lemon zest
 1/3 cup pistachios
 5 tbsp olive oil
 Juice from 1 orange, freshly squeezed
 1 cup mint
 1 cup parsley
 Salt and pepper to taste

Tips: Some models of air fryer only let you cook up to 30 minutes at a time. Simply let the lamb cook for 30 minutes and add another 15 minutes afterward. There are also various different types of mint you can use to change the flavor slightly, such as using water mint for a softer mint taste or peppermint for a much sharper mint flavor, or even chili mint, which has a slight spiciness to it.

Stuffed Pork Steaks

340°F
BAKE

PREP TIME: 10 MINUTES / COOKING TIME: 20 MINUTES / SERVES: 4

Juicy pork steaks stuffed with a garlic and swiss cheese filling.

FAMILY-BASED

Ingredients:
- 4 pork loin steaks
- 4 slices ham
- 4 tsp garlic, minced
- 2 pickles, chopped
- 6 slices swiss cheese
- ¾ cup olive oil
- 2 tbsp mustard (rough estimation)
- 2 Limes, juice and zest
- 1 Orange, juice and zest
- 1 cup cilantro, roughly chopped
- 1 cup mint, roughly chopped
- 1 tsp dried oregano
- 2 tsp cumin
- Salt and pepper to taste

Method:
1. Mix the juice and zest of the limes and orange with the garlic, oil, cilantro, mint, oregano, cumin, salt, and pepper in a food processor and blend well. Transfer the marinade to a shallow bowl.
2. Season the steaks with salt and pepper, and toss in the marinade to coat them thoroughly. Lay out the steaks on a clean working surface and spread each with a thin layer of mustard. Place 1 ½ slices of cheese and 1 slice of ham on each steak and top with the pickles. Roll the steaks as tightly as possible and secure with toothpicks.
3. Place the steaks in your air fryer and cook for 20 minutes.
4. Use tongs to remove the steaks and serve. Be careful of the toothpicks when eating.

Tips: When cooking, mustard is often used to give cheese a stronger, more mature flavor. If you aren't fond of this effect, simply leave out the mustard. If you do like it, you can use this trick with other cheesy dishes, such as melted cheese sandwiches and cheese sticks.

Braised Pork

PREP TIME: 40 MINUTES / COOKING TIME: 40 MINUTES / SERVES: 4

370°F
BAKE

This dish focuses on simple flavors and tender meat that will melt in your mouth. This recipe requires a pan or baking tray, but it would be simplest to use a regular frying pan with a detachable handle that will fit in your air fryer.

LONG-TERM

Ingredients:
  2 lbs pork loin roast, cubed
  2 cloves garlic, minced
  ½ yellow onion, chopped
  ½ lb red grapes
  ½ cup dry white wine
  2 cups chicken stock
  4 tbsp butter, melted
  2 tbsp flour
  1 sprig thyme
  1 bay leaf
  1 tsp thyme, finely chopped
  Salt and pepper to taste

Method:
1. Season your pork with salt and pepper, and rub with 2 tbsp of the melted butter. Place in your air fryer basket and cook for 8 minutes.
2. While the pork is cooking, heat up the rest of the butter in your frying pan over medium heat and fry the garlic and onion for 2 minutes. Stir in the wine, stock, flour, thyme, bay leaf, salt, and pepper and bring to a simmer. Take the pan off the heat.
3. Toss your pork cubes and grapes in the sauce and cook in your air fryer for 30 minutes.
4. Plate the pork with sides and top with the sauce and grapes.

Tips: The braising technique is designed specifically to make meat tender, and works great with tougher types of meat such as sirloin, short loin, and ribs.

Beef Curry

BEGINNER,
FAMILY-BASED,

Ingredients:
- 2 lbs beef steak, cubed
- 3 potatoes, cubed
- 2 small onions, roughly chopped
- 2 cloves garlic, minced
- 1 tbsp wine mustard
- 2 tbsp tomato sauce
- 10 oz canned coconut milk
- 2 tbsp olive oil
- 2 ½ tbsp curry powder
- Salt and pepper to taste

PREP TIME: 10 MINUTES / COOKING TIME: 45 MINUTES / SERVES: 4 - 6

A very flavorful, classic dish which found its origins in India. Full of spices and lovely aromas. This dish requires a deep pan or baking tray, but a regular pot that fits into your air fryer is simplest.

Method:
1. Heat up your oil in a pot over medium heat and fry your onions and garlic for 4 minutes. Stir in the potatoes and mustard and cook for another minute.
2. Stir in the beef, tomato sauce, coconut milk, curry powder, salt, and pepper. Place your pot in the air fryer and cook for 40 minutes.
3. Serve the curry as is or over rice.

Tips: There are various types of curry powder from which you can choose your favorite, giving you more control over the taste. For a more authentic taste, there are also various recipes on how to make your own curry powder. You can also add one or two curry leaves to the dish for a slightly stronger curry taste.

Crispy Lamb

PREP TIME: 10 MINUTES / COOKING TIME: 30 MINUTES / SERVES: 4

This dish is simple and easy, and it can be served with various different side dishes.

Method:
1. Mix the oil and garlic together. Season the lamb with salt and pepper, and brush the oil and garlic onto the lamb.
2. Mix the nuts, bread crumbs, and rosemary in a bowl. Dip the lamb into the egg, making sure it's coated thoroughly. Then dip the lamb into the bread crumbs.
3. Place the lamb in your air fryer basket and cook for 25 minutes. Increase the temperature to 400 ℉ and cook for another 5 minutes.
4. Use tongs to remove the lamb and serve immediately.

Tips: If you don't want to use store-bought bread crumbs, you can make your own very easily. Simply blend a few crustless slices of bread in a food processor. Spread the crumbs out on an oven tray and bake until golden brown. This won't work in the air fryer, as the crumbs are too light and might fly into the fan of the air fryer. You can also substitute the bread crumbs with crushed corn flakes for a slightly different taste and texture.

360°F
BAKE

BEGINNER,
FAMILY-BASED

Ingredients:
28 oz rack of lamb
1 garlic clove, minced
2 tbsp toasted macadamia nuts, crushed
1 tbsp bread crumbs
1 egg, whisked
1 tbsp olive oil
1 tbsp rosemary, chopped
Salt and pepper to taste

Beef Brisket with Onion Sauce

300°F BAKE

BEGINNER,
LONG-TERM,
FAMILY-BASED

Ingredients:
- 4 lb beef brisket
- 1 lb onion, chopped
- 1 lb sweet onion, chopped
- 1 lb celery, chopped
- 1 lb carrot, chopped
- 1 0z garlic, chopped
- 16 oz canned tomatoes, chopped
- 1 cup white vinegar
- 4 cups water
- 4 oz cooking oil
- 1 cup brown sugar
- 16 earl grey tea bags

PREP TIME: 10 MINUTES / COOKING TIME: 2 HOURS / SERVES: 6

A crisp, juicy brisket with a delicious onion sauce. This recipe requires a pot that will fit in your air fryer.

Method:
1. Place the water, regular onion, ½ lb celery, and carrots in your pot and bring to a simmer over medium heat. Season with salt and pepper, and add the brisket and 8 tea bags. Stir lightly and cook in your air fryer for 1 hour and 30 minutes.
2. Roughly half an hour before the brisket is done, start the sauce by heating up the cooking oil in a saucepan over medium heat. Add the sweet onion and sauté for 1o minutes.
3. Add the remaining celery, garlic, tomatoes, wine, sugar, salt, pepper, and remaining 8 tea bags and bring to simmer. Cover with a lid and cook for 10 minutes. Remove and discard the tea bags.
4. Slice the brisket on a cutting board and serve with the onion sauce drizzled over the slices.

Tips: If you want, you can cook the brisket without the sauce and use your own favorite sauce, or you can cook the onion sauce individually and use it together with other dishes. You can also add some sliced mushrooms to the sauce, or some cream to make the sauce a little thicker.

7

POULTRY DISHES

Chicken with Parsley Sauce

**380°F
FRY**

PREP TIME: 35 MINUTES / COOKING TIME: 25 MINUTES / SERVES: 6

**BEGINNER,
FAMILY-BASED**

A simple, easy recipe for chicken thighs, with a delicious herb sauce.

Ingredients:
 12 chicken thighs
 4 cloves garlic
 ½ cup olive oil
 ¼ cup red wine
 1 cup parsley
 1 tsp dried oregano
 Maple syrup
 Salt to taste

Method:
1. Mix the garlic, oil, wine, parsley, oregano, salt, and a small drizzle of maple syrup in a food processor and pulse until everything is mixed thoroughly, and transfer to a bowl.
2. Toss the chicken in the parsley sauce, making sure to completely coat all the pieces. Drain the chicken and gently pat dry with paper towels before placing in your air fryer basket. Cook for 25 minutes. Flip the chicken once.
3. Drizzle the remaining parsley sauce over the chicken and serve.

Tips: You can make the parsley sauce more or less sweet by adjusting the amount of maple syrup you use. You also have a lot of space to experiment with additional herbs for new flavors.

Southern Buttermilk-Fried Chicken

PREP TIME: 6 HOURS / COOKING TIME: 30 MINUTES / SERVES: 1

370°F
FRY

Marinated chicken breast with a crunchy, flavorful crust.

Method:

1. Mix the cayenne pepper, 2 tsp of pepper, and 1 tsp salt in a bowl. Toss the chicken breasts in the mixture and pour the buttermilk over the chicken. Make sure the chicken is completely coated and marinate in the refrigerator for at least six hours.
2. Make the mix for the coating by mixing the flour, baking powder, paprika, garlic powder, 1 tsp pepper, and 1 tsp salt in a bowl. Stir well to make sure the seasoning is spread evenly throughout the flour.
3. Working with one piece at a time, dip the marinated chicken in the seasoned flour. Make sure the chicken is coated thoroughly, but shake off any excess flour.
4. Place the chicken in your air fryer basket with the skin side facing upward and gently spray with some cooking oil. Cook for 20 minutes. Turn the chicken over and spray with cooking oil again. Cook for another 10 minutes.
5. Use tongs to remove the chicken and serve.

BEGINNER, BACHELOR, LONG-TERM

Ingredients:
- 2 chicken breasts
- 2 cups buttermilk
- 2 cups flour
- 1 tbsp baking powder
- 1 tbsp paprika
- 1 tsp cayenne pepper
- 1 tbsp garlic powder
- 3 tsp pepper
- 2 tsp salt
- Cooking oil

Tips: This recipe works well with drumsticks and wings as well, and is easy to adapt for larger quantities. It's also a good idea to prepare the chicken the night before and let it marinate overnight. If you know you'll prepare this meal again, you can mix a large amount of seasoned flour and keep it in an airtight container. As long as you store it in a cool, dry place, the flour will hold for months.

Tea Glazed Chicken

350°F
BAKE

A fruity, sweet dish with an interesting tea flavor. This dish requires a deep pan or baking tray.

BEGINNER

Ingredients:
- 6 chicken legs
- 1 onion, chopped
- ½ cup pineapple preserve
- ½ cup apricot preserve
- 1 tbsp soy sauce
- 1 tbsp olive oil
- 1 cup hot water
- ¼ tsp red pepper flakes
- 6 tea bags
- Salt and pepper to taste

Method:
1. Let the tea bags steep in the hot water for 10 minutes. Keep the water covered and on a stove over low heat to keep it warm. Discard the tea bags once done.
2. Mix the tea, pineapple and apricot preserve, soy sauce, and pepper flakes in a bowl. Stir well until the preserve dissolves and take off the heat.
3. Rub the chicken with the salt, pepper, and oil, and place in your air fryer basket. Cook the chicken for 5 minutes. Spread the chopped onion in your pan and add the chicken pieces. Drizzle the tea glaze over your chicken, making sure that all pieces are coated properly. Lower the temperature of your air fryer to 320 °F and cook for another 25 minutes.
4. Plate the chicken and cover with the onions and glaze. Serve while still hot.

Tips: The type of tea you use can have a large effect on the final result. Black tea will have a much stronger taste than green or white tea, and flavored teas will bring additional flavors to the table. You can also use six tsp loose tea. Simply use tea sieves or pour the tea through a filter once done steeping.

Marinated Duck Breasts

350°F
BAKE

A succulent, fatty poultry dish with a lovely, sticky, slightly sweet marinade.

Method:
1. Mix the garlic, soy sauce, wine, tarragon, salt, and pepper in a bowl. Toss the duck breasts in the marinade and keep refrigerated for a whole day.
2. Once done marinating, lightly pat the duck dry and place in your air fryer basket. Cook for 10 minutes, and turn the breasts over halfway through.
3. While the duck is cooking, heat the marinade in a saucepan over medium heat. Stir in the butter and sherry, and let it simmer for 5 minutes before taking it off the heat.
4. Drizzle the sauce over the duck and serve.

Did you know: The mallard breed of duck is most commonly used for cooking and has been domesticated as livestock in many cultures.

BEGINNER, LONG-TERM

Ingredients:
2 duck breasts
2 cloves garlic, minced
1 tbsp butter
¼ cup soy sauce
1 cup white wine
¼ cup sherry wine
6 sprigs tarragon
Salt and pepper to taste

Lemon Chicken

**350°F
BAKE**

BEGINNER,
FAMILY-BASED,
LONG-TERM

Ingredients:
- 1 chicken, cut into medium-sized pieces
- Zest and juice of 2 lemons
- 1 tbsp olive oil
- Salt and pepper to taste

PREP TIME: 10 MINUTES / COOKING TIME: 30 MINUTES / SERVES: 6

A simple, easy recipe with classic flavors.

Method:
1. Rub the chicken with the lemon zest, olive oil, salt, and pepper. Drizzle half the lemon juice over the chicken and turn the pieces over. Then drizzle the rest of the lemon juice.
2. Place the chicken in your air fryer basket and cook for 30 minutes. Turn the chicken over halfway through.
3. Use tongs to remove the chicken and serve with a fresh salad.

Tips: You can sprinkle the chicken with dried thyme or rosemary, put a few sprigs of fresh rosemary in the air fryer basket, or let the chicken rest in the lemon juice with a few herbs for additional taste.

Turkey Quarters and Vegetables

PREP TIME: 10 MINUTES / COOKING TIME: 34 MINUTES / SERVES: 4

360°F
BAKE

Juicy turkey cooked together with vegetables to absorb more flavor. This recipe requires a pan or baking tray.

BEGINNER,
FAMILY-BASED

Method:
1. Season the turkey with salt and pepper and rub with 1 tbsp olive oil, sage, rosemary, and thyme. Place the quarters in your air fryer basket and cook for 20 minutes.
2. Place the carrot, onion, celery, garlic, and bay leaves in your pan. Drizzle with the rest of the olive oil, pour over the stock, and season with salt and pepper. Add the turkey quarters and cook for another 14 minutes.
3. Plate the turkey and vegetables. Drizzle with the sauce in the pan and serve.

Ingredients:
   2 lb turkey quarters
   1 carrot, chopped
   1 onion, roughly chopped
   1 stalk celery, chopped
   3 cloves garlic, minced
   2 tbsp olive oil
   1 cup chicken stock
   ½ tsp dried sage
   ½ tsp dried rosemary
   ½ tsp dried thyme
   2 bay leaves
   Salt and pepper to taste

Tips: It's very easy to substitute in other vegetables like broccoli, sweet potatoes, pumpkin, potatoes, etc. If using potatoes, you should cook the potatoes slightly in the microwave beforehand, as they take longer than other vegetables to fully cook.

Chicken and Lentils Casserole

320°F
BAKE

LONG-TERM,
FAMILY-BASED

Ingredients:
- 2 lbs chicken breasts, deboned, skinned & chopped
- 1 ½ cups green lentils
- 2 red bell peppers, chopped
- 1 onion, chopped
- 2 cups corn
- 14 oz canned tomatoes, chopped
- 5 cloves garlic, minced
- 2 cups cheddar cheese, shredded
- 3 cups chicken stock
- Cooking oil
- 1 cup cilantro, chopped
- 3 tsp cumin, ground
- 1 tbsp garlic powder
- 2 tbsp jalapeno pepper, chopped (optional)
- Salt and cayenne pepper to taste

PREP TIME: 10 MINUTES / COOKING TIME: 1 HOUR / SERVES: 8

A filling, nutritious chicken casserole for the whole family to enjoy. This recipe requires a casserole dish that will fit inside your air fryer.

Method:
1. Heat up the stock and lentils in a pot over medium heat. Stir in salt and bring to a boil. Cook for 35 minutes.
2. While the lentils are cooking, lightly drizzle or spray the chicken with cooking oil. Season with 1 tsp cumin, salt, and cayenne pepper, and place in your air fryer basket. Cook for 6 minutes. Flip the chicken halfway through.
3. Place your chicken in your casserole dish and add the bell peppers, onion, tomatoes, garlic, 1 tsp cumin, and season with salt and cayenne pepper. Drain the lentils and add to the casserole dish. Mix thoroughly.
4. Add the corn, 1 cup cheese, garlic powder, the remaining cumin, and ½ cup cilantro. You can also add the jalapeno if you want. lower the temperature of your air fryer to 320 F and cook for 25 minutes.
5. Sprinkle the remaining cheese and cilantro over the casserole and serve.

Tips: Although it isn't strictly necessary, it might be beneficial to grease your casserole dish beforehand. You can also substitute the jalapeno with a very mild chili pepper if you want the additional taste but not the heat.

Duck with Cherries

PREP TIME: 10 MINUTES / COOKING TIME: 20 MINUTES / SERVES: 4

350°F
BAKE

Succulent duck breast with a tangy, slightly sweet cherry sauce. This recipe requires a frying pan that will fit in your air fryer and can be used on the stove.

BEGINNER

Method:
1. Season the duck with salt and pepper, and place in your air fryer basket. Cook for 10 minutes. Turn the duck over halfway through.
2. While the duck is cooking, heat up your pan and add the cherries, rhubarb, onion, jalapeno, ginger, honey, vinegar, sugar, sage, cloves, cinnamon, and cumin. Stir until the sugar dissolves. Bring to a simmer and cook for 10 minutes.
3. Toss the duck breast in the cherry sauce. Plate the duck and top with the cherries and rhubarb. Serve while still hot.

Ingredients:
- 4 duck breasts, with skin & scored
- 2 cups cherries, pitted
- 2 cups rhubarb, chopped
- ½ cup onion, chopped
- 1 jalapeno, chopped
- 1 tbsp ginger, grated
- ¼ cup honey
- 1/3 cup balsamic vinegar
- ½ cup sugar
- 4 sage leaves, chopped
- ½ tsp clove, ground
- ½ tsp cinnamon powder
- 1 tsp cumin, ground
- Salt and pepper to taste

Tips: The term "scored" simply means that the meat has shallow cuts made in its surface. This recipe works with duck legs as well, but keep in mind that the legs are much fattier than the breast.

Chinese Duck Legs

370°F
BAKE

BEGINNER,
BACHELOR

Ingredients:
- 2 duck legs
- 1 bunch spring onions, chopped
- 4 slices ginger
- 1 tbsp olive oil
- 1 tbsp sesame oil
- 1 tbsp rice wine
- 1 tbsp soy sauce
- 1 tbsp oyster sauce
- 14 oz water
- 2 star anise
- 2 dried chilies, chopped

PREP TIME: 10 MINUTES / COOKING TIME: 36 MINUTES / SERVES: 1 – 2

A traditional Chinese recipe for succulent duck legs with a spicy sauce. This dish requires a pan or baking tray, but a frying pan that will fit your air fryer will be simplest.

Method:
1. Heat the sesame and olive oil in your pan over medium heat and add the ginger, rice wine, soy sauce, oyster sauce, water, star anise, and dried chilies. Cook for 6 minutes.
2. Toss the duck legs and spring onions in the sauce, making sure everything is coated thoroughly. Move the pan to the air fryer and cook for 30 minutes.
3. Drizzle the duck legs and spring onions with the sauce when serving.

Tips: Rice wine may be tricky to get your hands on sometimes. Good substitutes for this ingredient are rice vinegar, white wine vinegar, or champagne vinegar.

8

VEGETABLES DISHES

Green Beans with Parmesan

390°F ROAST

BEGINNER,
FAST,
VEGETARIAN,
FAMILY-BASED

Ingredients:
12 oz green beans
1 egg, whisked
2 tsp garlic, minced
2 tbsp olive oil
1/3 cup parmesan
Salt and pepper to taste

PREP TIME: 8 MINUTES / COOKING TIME: 8 MINUTES / SERVES: 2 - 4

A simple, cheesy recipe that works well with other dishes.

Method:
1. Whisk the egg together with the garlic, oil, salt, and pepper. Toss the beans in the mix, coating them thoroughly, and sprinkle with parmesan.
2. Place the green beans in your air fryer basket and cook for 8 minutes.
3. Use tongs to remove the beans and serve immediately.

Tips: For additional taste, you can add some cayenne pepper and chopped herbs to the egg mix. You can also sprinkle the cooked beans with more cheese as a garnish when serving.

Swiss Chard Salad

PREP TIME: 10 MINUTES / COOKING TIME: 13 MINUTES / SERVES: 4

350°F
BAKE

A warm, healthy salad with a lovely vinaigrette and nuts for some extra crunch. This recipe requires a frying pan that will fit in your air fryer.

BEGINNER, VEGAN, FAMILY-BASED

Method:
1. In your frying pan, fry your chard and onion in the oil over medium heat for five minutes, or just until lightly browned and charred.
2. Take off the heat and add the raisins, pine nuts, vinegar, pepper flakes, salt, and pepper, and cook in your air fryer.
3. Plate the salad and serve while still warm.

Tips: You can substitute the swiss chard with spinach, bok choy, mustard greens, or black Tuscan kale. If you're using kale, you will need to increase the cooking time.

Ingredients:
- 1 bunch swiss chard, torn
- 1 small onion, roughly chopped
- ¼ cup raisins
- ¼ cup pine nuts, toasted
- 2 tbsp olive oil
- 1 tbsp balsamic vinegar
- Red pepper flakes to taste
- Salt and pepper to taste

Broccoli and Tomato Stew

**360°F
BAKE**

PREP TIME: 10 MINUTES / COOKING TIME: 20 MINUTES / SERVES: 2 - 4

A tasty vegetable stew. This dish requires a deep pan or baking tray, but a pot that fits in your air fryer will be simplest.

**BEGINNER,
VEGAN**

Method:

Ingredients:
- 1 head broccoli, separated into bite-size pieces
- 28 oz canned tomatoes, pureed
- 1 onion, roughly chopped
- 1 small piece ginger, chopped
- 1 clove garlic, minced
- 1 tbsp olive oil
- 2 tsp coriander seeds
- Crushed red pepper to taste
- Salt and pepper to taste

1. Fry the onion in oil over medium heat for 7 minutes. Season with salt and red and black pepper.
2. Remove from heat and add the broccoli, tomatoes, ginger, garlic, and coriander seeds. Cook in your air fryer for 12 minutes.
3. Serve while still warm.

Tips: You can add one or two tsp sugar to the stew to break the acidity of the tomatoes if you want. You can also experiment with fresh basil or parsley in the dish.

Zucchini Noodles Delight

PREP TIME: 10 MINUTES / COOKING TIME: 20 MINUTES / SERVES: 6

This dish is completely vegan but has a similar effect to spaghetti. This recipe requires a pan that will fit in your air fryer and can be used on the stove.

Method:
1. Season the zucchini noodles with salt and pepper and let them rest for 10 minutes.
2. In your pan, fry the garlic in the oil over medium heat for 1 minute. Remove from heat and add the zucchini, spinach, mushrooms, sun-dried tomatoes, cherry tomatoes, and tomato sauce. Stir well and cook in the air fryer for 10 minutes.
3. Garnish with basil and serve.

Tips: For a bit of a fresher taste, you can add the cherry tomatoes after cooking rather than before cooking.

320°F
BAKE

BEGINNER,
VEGAN,
FAMILY-BASED

Ingredients:
3 zucchinis, cut into thin, spaghetti-like strips
2 cups spinach, torn
16 oz mushrooms, sliced
1 tsp garlic, minced
¼ cup sun-dried tomatoes, chopped
½ cup cherry tomatoes, halved
2 tbsp olive oil
2 cups tomato sauce
Salt and pepper to taste
Chopped basil

Sweet Potato Mix

350°F
BAKE

PREP TIME: 10 MINUTES / COOKING TIME: 15 MINUTES / SERVES: 4

Cooked sweet potatoes and a fresh dressing, with a bit of bacon for extra crunch.

BEGINNER,
FAMILY-BASED

Method:
1. Toss your sweet potatoes and bacon in the garlic and 2 tbsp olive oil, coating everything thoroughly. Place in your air fryer basket and cook for 15 minutes.

Ingredients:
- 3 sweet potatoes, cubed
- ½ lb bacon, roughly chopped
- 4 cloves garlic, minced
- 2 green onions, chopped
- 4 tbsp olive oil
- Juice from 1 lime
- 2 tbsp balsamic vinegar
- Cinnamon powder
- Dill, chopped
- Red pepper flakes to taste
- Salt and pepper to taste

2. Mix the onions, remaining oil, lime juice, vinegar, a dash of cinnamon powder, a handful of dill, pepper flakes, salt, and pepper in a bowl and whisk together.
3. Drizzle the dressing over the sweet potatoes and bacon and serve.

Tips: You can leave out the bacon for a vegan version of this dish. You can also add some chopped nuts for additional taste and texture.

Spinach Pie

PREP TIME: 10 MINUTES / COOKING TIME: 15 MINUTES / SERVES: 4

Rich spinach pies that can work well as a full or light meal and go well with other sides. This dish requires 4 small ramekins.

**360°F
BAKE**

BEGINNER,
VEGETARIAN,
FAMILY-BASED

Method:
1. Mix 1 egg, butter, milk, flour, salt, and pepper in a food processor and blend well. Place in a bowl and knead until a crumbly dough forms. Cover the dough and let rest for 10 minutes.
2. Fry the spinach and onion in the oil over medium heat for 2 minutes. Stir in the cottage cheese, remaining egg, salt, and pepper, and take off the heat.
3. Divide the dough into 4 equal pieces and roll out on a clean working surface. Place each sheet of dough on the bottom of a greased ramekin. Fill the ramekins with the spinach filling and place in your air fryer basket. Bake for 15 minutes. It may be necessary to bake the pies in batches.
4. Use tongs to remove the ramekins and serve while still warm.

Ingredients:
7 oz spinach
1 medium onion, chopped
2 oz cottage cheese
2 eggs
1 tbsp olive oil
2 tbsp butter
2 tbsp milk
7 oz flour
Salt and pepper to taste

Tips: You can add some cayenne pepper to the filling for some extra flavor. It's also possible to bake one large pie rather than four smaller ones as long as the ramekin will fit in your air fryer basket.

Portobello Mushrooms

350°F
BAKE

PREP TIME: 10 MINUTES / COOKING TIME: 12 MINUTES / SERVES: 2 – 4

Portobello mushrooms stuffed with a healthy, nutty filling.

**BEGINNER,
BACHELOR,
VEGAN**

Ingredients:
- 4 portobello mushrooms, stems removed and chopped
- 1 cup baby spinach
- 8 cherry tomatoes, halved
- 3 cloves garlic, chopped
- 1 cup almonds, roughly chopped
- ¼ cup olive oil
- 1 tbsp parsley
- 10 basil leaves
- Salt and pepper to taste

Method:
1. Season the chopped mushroom stems with salt and pepper and blend together with the spinach, tomatoes, garlic, almonds, oil, parsley, and basil in a food processor.
2. Stuff each mushroom with this filling and place in your air fryer basket. Cook for 12 minutes. It may be necessary to cook the mushrooms in batches.
3. Use tongs to remove the mushrooms and serve while still warm.

Tips: You can experiment with different fillings for the mushrooms, such as basil or tomato pesto, etc. You can also add garnishes after cooking, such as grated cheese, chopped nuts, or fresh herbs.

Mexican Peppers

Roasted bell peppers stuffed with spicy chicken and jalapeno. This recipe requires a pan or baking tray.

Method:
1. Mix the chicken breast, tomatoes, onion, green pepper, jalapeno, tomato juice, tomato sauce, chili powder, cumin, onion powder, red pepper, garlic powder, salt, and pepper in your pan. Stir thoroughly and cook for 15 minutes.
2. Using 2 forks, shred the chicken. Stir the mix well, and stuff into the bell peppers. Place the bell peppers in your air fryer basket, turn the temperature down to 320 ℉ and cook for 10 minutes.
3. Use tongs to remove the peppers and serve.

Tips: You can substitute the chicken with ground beef or pork and mix in cooked beans. You can also add some gouda or mozzarella cheese when stuffing the peppers and top with some fresh chopped parsley or rosemary. If the stuffing is too spicy, you can remove the jalapeno, chili powder, and/or red pepper.

320°F
BAKE

BEGINNER,
BACHELOR

Ingredients:
   4 bell peppers, tops
      cut off, seeded
   4 chicken breasts
   1 cup tomatoes,
      chopped
   ¼ cup onion, finely
      chopped
   ¼ cup green
      peppers, chopped
   2 tbsp jarred
      jalapeno, chopped
   ½ cup tomato juice
   2 cups tomato
      sauce
   1 tsp chili powder
   1 tsp cumin,
      ground
   2 tsp onion powder
   ½ tsp red pepper,
      crushed
   ½ tsp garlic powder
   Salt and pepper to
   taste

Broccoli Hash

350°F
BAKE

A green, less starchy alternative to hash browns.

BEGINNER,
BACHELOR,
VEGETARIAN

Ingredients:
  1 broccoli head,
    florets separated
  10 oz mushrooms,
    halved
  1 onion, chopped
  1 avocado, peeled
    & cut into chunks
  1 clove garlic,
    minced
  1 tbsp olive oil
  1 tbsp balsamic
    vinegar
  1 tsp dried basil
  Red pepper flakes
    to taste
  Salt and pepper to
  taste

Method:
  1. Mix the broccoli, mushroom, onion, avocado, and garlic in a bowl, stirring well.
  2. Mix the oil, vinegar, basil, salt, and pepper in a separate bowl and whisk thoroughly. Pour this mix over the broccoli mix, making sure everything is coated. Let rest for 30 minutes. Once done resting, place in your air fryer basket and cook for 8 minutes.
  3. Season with red pepper flakes and serve.

Tips: The avocado is added to give the hash a creamier texture. If you don't want this, you can simply leave out the avocado. A good serving tip is to plate a soft fried egg on top of the hash, letting the runny egg yolk work as a sauce.

9

SIDE DISHES

Brussels Sprouts

PREP TIME: 10 MINUTES / COOKING TIME: 15 MINUTES / SERVES: 4

Fried brussels sprouts with a fresh mayonnaise dressing.

BEGINNER,
VEGETARIAN,
FAMILY-BASED

Ingredients:
- 1 lb brussels sprouts, trimmed & halved
- 2 tbsp roasted garlic, crushed
- ½ cup mayonnaise
- 6 tsp olive oil
- ½ tsp thyme, chooped
- Salt and pepper to taste

Method:
1. Season your brussels sprouts with salt and pepper, and coat with oil. Place in your air fryer basket and cook for 15 minutes.
2. In the meantime, mix the garlic, mayonnaise, and thyme in a bowl and whisk together.
3. Use tongs to remove the brussels sprouts and top with a dollop of mayonnaise dressing when serving.

Did you know: There are various easy recipes on how to make your own mayonnaise using egg yolks and vegetable oil as the main ingredients.

Mushrooms and Sour Cream

PREP TIME: 10 MINUTES / COOKING TIME: 10 MINUTES / SERVES: 4 - 6

360°F
BAKE

Roasted mushrooms with a sour cream filling and topped with cheese. This dish goes great with most other dishes.

BEGINNER, FAMILY-BASED

Method:
1. Fry the bacon, bell pepper, onion, and carrot over medium heat in a frying pan for 1 minute. Season with salt and pepper and add the sour cream. Cook for another minute and take off the heat. Let the filling cool down.
2. Stuff the mushrooms with the filling and top with cheese. Place the mushrooms in your air fryer basket and cook for 8 minutes.
3. Serve while still warm.

Ingredients:
24 mushrooms, stems removed
2 bacon strips, finely chopped
1 green bell pepper, finely chopped
1 medium onion, finely chopped
1 carrot, grated
1 cup cheddar cheese, grated
½ cup sour cream
Salt and pepper to taste

Tips: For some extra flavor, you can add chopped chives to the sour cream stuffing or garnish the mushrooms with the chives when serving.

Onion Rings

360°F
BAKE

BEGINNER,
VEGETARIAN,
FAMILY-BASED

Ingredients:
- 2 onions, sliced into medium-sized rings
- 2 cups milk
- 2 eggs
- 2 ½ cups flour
- 2 tsp baking powder
- 1 ½ cups bread crumbs
- Salt

A classic side dish that always goes well with french fries and dipping sauces.

Method:
1. Mix the flour, baking powder, and a pinch of salt in a shallow bowl. Coat the onion rings in the flour mixture and place them on a separate plate.
2. Add the milk and eggs to the flour mix. Dip the onion rings in the batter and coat them thoroughly with the bread crumbs. Place the onion rings in your air fryer basket and cook for 10 minutes.
3. Use tongs to remove the onion rings and serve.

Tips: For extra flavor, you can add some cayenne pepper or chopped herbs to the flour mix. You can also add grated mozzarella for an effect slightly similar to cheese sticks.

Cheddar Biscuits

PREP TIME: 10 MINUTES / COOKING TIME: 20 MINUTES / SERVES: 2 – 4

380°F
BAKE

Simple, cheese flavored biscuits that go great with saucy foods or salads.

BEGINNER,
BACHELOR,
VEGETARIAN

Method:
1. Mix the cheese, ½ cup butter, buttermilk, self-rising flour, and sugar in a bowl until the ingredients form a dough.
2. Sprinkle the flour over a clean surface. Roll the dough out and use a cookie cutter to cut out approximately 8 circles. Coat the circles with flour.
3. Line your air fryer basket with foil and place the biscuits inside in a single layer, and brush them with the melted butter. Bake for 20 minutes. It may be necessary to bake the biscuits in batches.
4. Use tongs to remove the biscuits and let them cool before serving.

Ingredients:
½ cup cheddar cheese, grated
½ cup butter, 1 tbsp melted butter
1 ⅓ cups buttermilk
2 ⅓ cups self-rising flour
1 cup flour
2 tbsp sugar

Tips: Although they are meant as a side, these biscuits work well as a snack. This recipe can easily be adapted for larger quantities, and the biscuits can be stored in an airtight container for up to a week.

Eggplant Fries

400°F ROAST

BEGINNER,
FAST,
BACHELOR,
VEGETARIAN

Ingredients:
- 1 eggplant, peeled & cut into medium wedges
- 1 egg, whisked
- ½ cup Italian cheese, shredded
- 2 tbsp milk
- 2 cups panko bread crumbs
- Salt and pepper to taste

PREP TIME: 10 MINUTES / COOKING TIME: 5 MINUTES / SERVES: 2 - 4

This is a tasty alternative to french fries, with eggplant wedges dipped in a cheesy crust.

Method:
1. Whisk the egg, milk, salt, and pepper in a shallow bowl. In a separate bowl, mix the cheese and bread crumbs, and stir well.
2. Dip the eggplant wedges in the egg mix, and then in the cheese and crumb mix, making sure that both layers coat the eggplant properly. Grease your air fryer basket and place the eggplant fries inside. Cook for 5 minutes.
3. Use tongs to remove the fries and serve.

Tips: You can substitute the eggplant with zucchini, which will have a less prominent taste but similar texture. You can also add a bit of cayenne pepper or chopped herbs such as parsley or thyme to the crumb mix for extra flavor.

Cauliflower Rice

PREP TIME: 10 MINUTES / COOKING TIME: 40 MINUTES / SERVES: 4

350°F
BAKE

A vegetarian alternative to dirty rice, made with mushrooms and chestnuts, and which goes well with most types of main dish. This recipe requires a deep pan or baking tray.

BEGINNER, VEGETARIAN, FAMILY BASED

Method:
1. Stir the cauliflower, garlic, ginger, soy sauce, sesame oil, peanut oil, and lemon juice together in your pan. Cover with a heat resistant lid and cook for 20 minutes.
2. Add the mushrooms, peas, chestnuts, and egg, mixing well. Increase the temperature of your air fryer to 360 °F and cook for another 20 minutes.
3. Serve together with your favorite dishes.

Tips: You can substitute the egg with products like egg-replacer, ground flax seeds, or flegg, for a completely vegan dish. You can also simply leave out the egg, but the rice will not stick together as well and will be a little less dense.

Ingredients:
- 1 head cauliflower, riced
- 15 oz mushrooms, chopped
- ¾ cup peas
- 3 garlic cloves, minced
- 9 oz water chestnuts, drained
- 1 tbsp ginger, grated
- 1 egg, whisked
- 4 tbsp soy sauce
- 1 tbsp sesame oil
- 1 tbsp peanut oil
- ½ Lemon, juice

Mushroom Cakes

400°F
FRY

PREP TIME: 10 MINUTES / COOKING TIME: 8 MINUTES / SERVES: 4 - 8

Crispy, fried mushroom cakes bursting with flavor that go especially well with meaty dishes like steak.

VEGETARIAN, FAMILY-BASED

Ingredients:
- 4 oz mushrooms, chopped
- 1 onion, finely chopped
- 1 tbsp butter
- 2 tbsp olive oil
- 14 oz milk
- 1 tbsp bread crumbs
- 1 ½ tbsp flour
- ½ tsp nutmeg, ground
- Salt and pepper to taste

Method:
1. Fry the mushrooms and onion in the butter over medium heat in a frying pan for 3 minutes. Stir in the flour and remove from the heat.
2. Keep stirring the mixture while gradually adding the milk. Add the nutmeg and season with salt and pepper. Mix well and let the mix cool down completely.
3. Mix the oil and bread crumbs in a bowl. One spoonful at a time, add the mushroom mix to the bread crumb mix and form a small patty-like cake. Make sure the mushroom mix is properly coated. Place the cakes in your air fryer basket and cook for 8 minutes.
4. Use tongs to remove the cakes and serve.

Did you know: You can freeze the mushroom cakes both before and after cooking. If freezing leftover patties that have been cooked already, let them cool down fully before freezing and drizzle with a little oil when reheating. Don't freeze or refrigerate the patties after reheating them once.

Roasted Parsnips

PREP TIME: 10 MINUTES / COOKING TIME: 40 MINUTES / SERVES: 6

A very simple recipe for parsnips roasted in syrup, which can work as a great counter with acidic or very rich dishes. This recipe requires a pan or baking tray.

Method:
1. Heat up the oil in your pan in the air fryer, giving the air fryer a chance to preheat. Add the parsnip chunks, maple syrup, and parsley flakes. Make sure the parsnip is fully coated and cook for 40 minutes.
2. Serve while still warm.

Tips: This recipe also works well with carrots, turnips, sweet potatoes, butternut, and parsley root, though the texture may vary slightly depending on the ingredient. You can substitute the parsley flakes with dried rosemary, or a sprig or two of fresh rosemary. You can also adjust how sweet the dish is by altering the amount of maple syrup.

360°F
ROAST

BEGINNER, VEGETARIAN, FAMILY-BASED

Ingredients:
- 2 lbs parsnips, peeled & cut into medium-sized chunks
- 1 tbsp olive oil
- 2 tbsp maple syrup
- 1 tbsp dried parsley flakes

Creamy Cabbage

PREP TIME: 10 MINUTES / COOKING TIME: 20 MINUTES / SERVES: 4

A rich, creamy side dish with bacon for extra flavor, which is simple and easy to prepare. This recipe requires a pan or baking tray.

BEGINNER,
FAMILY-BASED

Method:
1. Mix the cream, cornstarch, salt, and pepper in a bowl, stirring well. Place your cabbage, onion, and bacon in your pan and drizzle with the cream.
2. Make sure the cabbage is properly coated and cook for 20 minutes.
3. Plate while still warm.

Ingredients:
 1 head green cabbage, chopped
 1 medium onion, chopped
 4 slices bacon, chopped
 1 cup whipped cream
 2 tbsp cornstarch
 Salt and pepper to taste

Tips: If you want to make sure your bacon is extra crispy, fry it for a minute or two in a bit of oil beforehand. You can either do this on the stove or in the air fryer. To give your dish different tastes, you can add a small amount of wine, cayenne pepper, or your favorite herbs to the cream.

Pumpkin Rice

PREP TIME: 5 MINUTES/ COOKING TIME: 30 MINUTES /
SERVES: 4

360°F
BAKE

A very simple, aromatic rice dish with pumpkin puree and cream. This recipe requires a heat resistant dish that will fit in your air fryer.

BEGINNER,
FAMILY-BASED

Method:
1. Mix the rice, pumpkin puree, onion, garlic, ginger, oil, stock, cream, thyme, allspice, nutmeg, and cinnamon powder in your dish. Make sure all the ingredients are thoroughly mixed and cook for 30 minutes. If the only dish that fits in your air fryer is too small for all the ingredients, you will have to divide the ingredients and cook the rice in batches.
2. Serve while still warm.

Tips: You can substitute the chicken stock with vegetable stock for a completely vegetarian dish. If you want more fiber and protein in the dish, you can substitute the white rice with brown rice, but you will have to add more stock or cream and extend the cooking time. The best way to see exactly how to do this is to compare the fluid to rice ratio and cooking times on the packaging of the white and brown rice. Furthermore, there are various recipes available on how to make your own allspice

Ingredients:
- 12 oz white rice
- 6 oz pumpkin puree
- 1 small onion, chopped
- 2 cloves garlic, minced
- ½ tsp ginger, grated
- 2 tbsp olive oil
- 4 cups chicken stock
- 4 oz heavy cream
- 1 tsp thyme, chopped
- ½ tsp allspice
- ½ tsp nutmeg
- ½ tsp cinnamon powder

10

DESSERTS

Cheesecake

VEGETARIAN,
LONG-TERM,
FAMILY-BASED

Ingredients:
- 1 lb cream cheese
- 2 eggs
- ½ tsp vanilla extract
- 2 tbsp butter
- 1 cup graham crackers, crumbled
- 4 tbsp sugar

PREP TIME: 10 MINUTES / COOKING TIME: 15 MINUTES / SERVES: 15

A simple, straightforward baked cheesecake the whole family will enjoy. This recipe requires a lined cake pan that will fit in your air fryer.

Method:
1. Mix the crackers and butter in a bowl until it forms a crumble. Press the crumble onto the bottom of your cake pan, and bake for 4 minutes.
2. Mix the cream cheese, eggs, vanilla extract, and sugar in a bowl and whisk well. Pour the filling over the crust in your pan and spread evenly. Lower your air fryer's temperature to 310 F and bake for 15 minutes.
3. Let the cake cool down completely and refrigerate for at least 3 hours before serving.

Tips: Because this recipe is so simple, you have a lot of space to play and experiment. You can add crushed nuts to the crust, or you can add ingredients to the filling, such as chocolate chips, lemon juice, berries, or lemon or orange zest. You can further garnish the cake with these additions when serving.

Banana Bread

PREP TIME: 10 MINUTES / COOKING TIME: 40 MINUTES / SERVES: 6

Another classic dessert, suitable for any occasion. This recipe requires a cake or bread pan that will fit in your air fryer.

Method:
1. Mix the bananas, butter, milk, vanilla, cream of tartar, and sugar in a bowl, stirring well. In a separate bowl, mix the flour, baking powder, and baking soda.
2. Gradually add the flour mixture to the banana mixture, stirring well to prevent clots. Grease your pan and pour in the batter. Bake for 40 minutes.
3. Let the bread cool down completely before trying to remove it from the pan. Slice and serve.

Tips: This recipe is a great way to use up bananas that are on the verge of being overripe. This recipe is also great for freezing. Simply wrap the bread in aluminum foil or thick plastic and freeze. It's best to use the bread within two to three months when it's still at its freshest, but it will last longer than that if stored properly.

320°F
BAKE

BEGINNER,
VEGETARIAN,
FAMILY-BASED

Ingredients:
2 bananas, mashed
1/3 cup butter
1/3 cup milk
1 egg
1 tsp vanilla extract
1 ½ tsp cream of tartar
1 ½ cups flour
1 tsp baking powder
½ tsp baking soda
¾ cup sugar

Crispy Apples

BEGINNER,
BACHELOR,
VEGETARIAN

Ingredients:
    5 apples, cored &
        cut into medium-
        sized chunks
    ¾ cup rolled oats
    4 tbsp butter
    1 tbsp maple syrup
    ½ cup water
    ¼ cup brown sugar
    ¼ cup flour
    2 tsp cinnamon
        powder
    ½ tsp nutmeg
        powder
    Salt

PREP TIME: 10 MINUTES / COOKING TIME: 10 MINUTES /
SERVES: 2 – 4

An apple pudding that goes well with a dollop of whipped
cream. This dish requires a deep pan or baking tray.

Method:
1. Mix the apples, maple syrup, water, cinnamon, and
   nutmeg, stirring well. Toss to make sure the apple
   chunks are thoroughly coated.
2. Mix the oats, butter, sugar, and flour in a bowl. Add
   a dash of salt and mix well. Drop the oat mixture
   into the pan, on top of the apples, in spoonfuls. Bake
   for 10 minutes.
3. Serve while still warm.

Did you know: The type of apple you use will have a slight
effect on your dish. Granny Smith apples will have a softer,
more subtle taste and flavor, while crisp green apples will
be much crispier and your dessert will have a faint hint of
sourness to it.

Carrot and Pineapple Bread

PREP TIME: 10 MINUTES / COOKING TIME: 45 MINUTES / SERVES: 6

**320°F
BAKE**

A lovely vegan dessert that can work great as a tea time snack as well. This dish requires a springform pan that will fit into your air fryer.

BEGINNER,
VEGAN,
FAMILY-BASED

Method:
1. Mix the flour, baking powder, baking soda, nutmeg, cinnamon, and a dash of salt in a bowl. Stir well. In a separate bowl, mix the carrot, coconut flakes, pecans, coconut cream, pineapple juice, oil, flax meal, flour, and sugar. Stir well to prevent clumps.
2. Stir the carrot mixture into the flour batter and mix well. Grease your cake pan and pour in the batter. Cook for 45 minutes.
3. Let the cake cool before removing from the pan and serving.

Tips: A good way to add extra flavor and texture into the cake is to add pineapple pieces or crushed pineapple to the batter. You can also garnish with whipped cream and more nuts when serving.

Ingredients:
- 1/3 cup carrots, grated
- 1/3 cup coconut flakes, shredded
- 1/3 cup pecans, toasted & chopped
- 3 tbsp coconut cream
- ¼ cup pineapple juice
- 4 tbsp sunflower oil
- 1 tbsp flax meal, mixed with 2 tbsp water
- 5 oz whole wheat flour
- ½ cup sugar
- ¾ tsp baking powder
- ½ tsp baking soda
- ¼ tsp nutmeg, ground
- ½ tsp cinnamon powder
- Salt

Mini Lava Cakes

320°F
BAKE

PREP TIME: 10 MINUTES / COOKING TIME: 20 MINUTES / SERVES: 3

**BEGINNER,
BACHELOR,
VEGETARIAN**

Ingredients:
- 1 egg
- ½ tsp orange zest
- 4 tbsp milk
- 2 tbsp cooking oil
- 4 tbsp flour
- 4 tbsp sugar
- ½ tsp baking powder
- 1 tbsp cocoa powder

A lovely, decadent chocolate cake with a gooey center, often served with a small dollop of whipped cream or ice cream. This dish requires ramekins.

Method:
1. Mix the egg, orange zest, milk, oil, flour, sugar, baking powder, and cocoa powder together in a bowl. Stir well and make sure there are no clumps. Grease three ramekins very thoroughly and divide the batter. Bake for 20 minutes.
2. To remove the cakes from the ramekins, use a thin butter knife to loosen the edges of the cakes. Place the serving plate upside down over the ramekin, press the two together tightly and turn both over quickly so that the plate is on the bottom. Gently tap the base of the ramekin to loosen the cake more, and carefully lift the ramekin. The cake should slip out fairly easily.
3. Serve the cake while still warm.

Tips: If you are uncomfortable with removing the cake, you can serve it still inside the ramekin. You can also dust the greased ramekins with cocoa powder to help prevent the cake from sticking to the ramekins. Lava cakes are another dessert that is great to freeze and reheat again later.

Strawberry Doughnuts

PREP TIME: 10 MINUTES / COOKING TIME: 15 MINUTES / SERVES: 4

360°F BAKE

This is a recipe for plain, sweet doughnuts, with a delectable strawberry frosting.

Method:

1. Mix 1 tbsp butter, flour, white sugar, brown sugar, and baking powder in a bowl. In a separate bowl, mix 1 ½ tbsp butter, egg, and milk together and whisk well. Gradually pour the flour mixture into the egg mixture, stirring continuously to avoid clumps. Stir well until you have a smooth batter.
2. Form four doughnut rings and place them in your air fryer basket in a single layer. Bake for 15 minutes. The doughnuts should have space to rise a little, so it might be necessary to bake the doughnuts in batches.
3. While the doughnuts are baking, make your frosting by mixing the strawberries, remaining 2 tbsp butter, whipped cream, icing sugar, and food coloring in a bowl and whisk well.
4. Spread the frosting over the doughnuts and serve with some fresh strawberries.

BEGINNER, VEGETARIAN, FAMILY BASED

Ingredients:
- ¼ cup strawberries, finely chopped
- 1 tbsp whipped cream
- 4 ½ tbsp butter
- 1 egg
- 4 oz whole milk
- 8 oz flour
- 1 tbsp white sugar
- 1 tbsp brown sugar
- 3.5 oz icing sugar
- 1 tsp baking powder
- ½ tsp pink food coloring

Tips: This is another recipe that gives you a chance to experiment. You can substitute the strawberries with various other fruits and berries like blueberries, raspberries, peaches, cranberries, etc. You can even replace the strawberries with orange juice and chocolate shavings. Further, you can bake just the doughnuts and use your own favorite frosting, or you can use just the frosting on other baked goodies.

Wrapped Pears

PREP TIME: 10 MINUTES / COOKING TIME: 15 MINUTES / SERVES: 4

320°F
BAKE

BEGINNER,
VEGETARIAN,
FAMILY-BASED

Pear halves with a custard filling and wrapped with puff pastry.

Ingredients:
- 2 pears, halved
- 4 puff pastry sheets
- 14 oz vanilla custard
- 1 egg, whisked
- 2 tbsp sugar
- ½ tsp cinnamon powder

Method:
1. Lay out the pastry sheets on a clean working surface. Divide the custard between the sheets, keeping the custard away from the edges. Place the pear halves in the center, and fold the corners of the pastry over the pears to wrap them.
2. Brush the pastry with the whisked egg and sprinkle with sugar and cinnamon powder. Place the wrapped pears in your air fryer basket and bake for 15 minutes.
3. Serve while still warm with a dollop of whipped cream.

Tips: You can substitute the pears with apples for a different taste. There are also various recipes available on how to make your own custard.

Special Brownies

PREP TIME: 10 MINUTES / COOKING TIME: 17 MINUTES / SERVES: 2 - 4

A classic brownie recipe with a bit of a twist. This recipe requires a shallow cake pan that will fit in your air fryer.

Method:
1. Heat up 6 tbsp butter and the sugar over medium heat in a frying pan, and cook for 5 minutes. Meanwhile, mix the walnuts, vanilla extract, flour, and baking powder in a bowl. Add the butter and sugar to the mix and stir until you have a batter. Pour the batter into your greased pan.
2. In a separate bowl, mix the remaining butter and peanut butter and microwave for a few seconds. Stir thoroughly and pour over the brownie batter. Bake for 17 minutes.
3. Let the brownies cool down before cutting and serving.

Tips: To make the brownies even more special, you can add whole nuts, halved pecan nuts, or chocolate squares or chips to the dish before baking.

320°F
BAKE

VEGETARIAN,
BACHELOR

Ingredients:
- 1 egg
- 7 tbsp butter
- 1 tbsp peanut butter
- ¼ cups walnuts, chopped
- ½ tsp vanilla extract
- ¼ cup flour
- 1/3 cup sugar
- 1/3 cup cocoa powder
- ½ tsp baking powder

Orange Cake

330°F
BAKE

BEGINNER,
VEGAN,
FAMILY-BASED

Ingredients:
- ½ cup orange zest, grated
- ¾ cup orange juice
- 3 tbsp coconut oil, melted
- ½ cup pecans, chopped
- ½ cup raisins
- ½ cup almond milk
- 1 cup almond flour
- ¾ cup water
- 1 cup coconut sugar
- 1 tsp baking powder
- ¼ tsp cinnamon powder

PREP TIME: 10 MINUTES / COOKING TIME: 30 MINUTES / SERVES: 4

A healthy, tropical orange cake filled with nuts and coconut that will have the whole family happy. This dish requires a cake pan that will fit in your air fryer.

Method:
1. Mix 2 tbsp coconut oil, pecans, raisins, milk, flour, ½ cup sugar, baking powder, and cinnamon powder in a bowl. Stir well to form a batter. Grease your cake pan and pour in the batter.
2. In a frying pan, heat up the orange zest and juice, 1 tbsp coconut oil, water, and the remaining sugar over medium heat. Stir until the sugar is dissolved and bring to a boil. Pour the syrup over the batter and bake for 30 minutes.
3. Let the cake cool down and serve.

Did you know: Orange and chocolate are a very good combination, especially in Spanish cooking, so adding some chocolate chips or shavings to the batter, or garnishing the cake with a nice dark chocolate sauce, can be a great way to add to this dessert.

Lemon Tart

PREP TIME: 1 HOUR, 30 MINUTES / COOKING TIME: 35 MINUTES / SERVES: 4 – 6

360°F
BAKE

A lovely, buttery baked crust with a lemon filling, a close cousin of the key lime pie. This dish requires a tart pan that will fit in your air fryer.

LONG-TERM, VEGETARIAN, FAMILY-BASED

Method:
1. Mix the flour, 2 tbsp sugar, and a dash of salt, stirring well. Rub in the 12 tbsp cold butter, add the water, and knead until you have a dough. Form the dough into a ball, wrap with foil and keep refrigerated for 1 hour.
2. Roll the dough out on a floured work surface and place into the bottom of your tart pan. Use a fork to prick the dough a few times and refrigerate for another 20 minutes. Bake for 15 minutes.
3. While the tart base bakes, mix the melted butter, eggs, 1 ½ cup sugar, and lemon zest and juice in a bowl and whisk well. Pour the filling into your tart pan and spread evenly over the crust. Bake for 20 minutes.
4. Cut and serve the pie.

Ingredients:
12 tbsp cold butter
10 tbsp butter,
   melted & chilled
2 eggs, whisked
Zest from 2 lemons
Juice from 2
   lemons
3 tbsp ice water
2 cups flour
1 ½ cups & 2 tbsp
   sugar
Salt

Tips: As a variation, you can whisk custard powder into the filling to bake a lemon custard pie, or you can make a meringue by whisking egg whites and castor sugar to top the pie before baking to make a lemon meringue pie.

Banana Jamaica

370°F
BAKE

BEGINNER,
VEGETARIAN,
FAMILY-BASED

Ingredients:
- 8 bananas, halved lengthwise
- Juice from 2 oranges, freshly squeezed
- 2 tsp rum
- ½ cup brown sugar
- ½ tsp nutmeg, ground
- ¼ tsp cinnamon powder
- 1 quart vanilla ice cream

PREP TIME: 5 MINUTES / COOKING TIME: 24 MINUTES / SERVES: 8

A tropical banana sauce to pour over ice cream, bringing the contrasting hot and cold together in a refreshing dessert. This dish requires a deep pan or baking tray.

Method:
1. Place the bananas in your pan or baking tray. Mix the orange juice, rum, sugar, nutmeg, and cinnamon powder in a bowl and stir well.
2. Pour the orange juice mixture into the pan, making sure the bananas are thoroughly coated. Cook for 24 minutes.
3. Scoop the ice cream into bowls and pour the sauce and bananas over as soon as it's done cooking. Serve immediately.

Tips: If you want to cook this recipe without any alcohol, you can substitute the rum with rum essence. You can use thin lemon slices or cinnamon sticks as a garnish.

CONVERSION TABLES

The various recipes all over the world use different measuring units, temperature formats, and metric systems. This can sometimes be confusing and make it difficult to follow a foreign recipe. To help make it a little easier, here are tables that show how these temperatures and measuring units can be converted.

Temperatures

FAHRENHEIT	CELCIUS	COMMON DESCRIPTION
200 ℉	90 ℃	Cool oven
250 ℉	120 ℃	Very slow oven
300 - 325 ℉	150 - 160 ℃	Slow oven/Low heat
325 - 350 ℉	160 - 180 ℃	Moderately slow oven
350 - 375 ℉	180 - 190 ℃	Moderate oven/Medium heat
375 - 400 ℉	190 - 200 ℃	Moderately hot oven
400 - 450 ℉	200 - 230 ℃	Hot oven/High heat
450 - 500 ℉	230 - 260 ℃	Very hot oven/Fast oven

Volume conversions (liquid based)

UNIT	STANDARD US	METRIC (ROUNDED)	COMMON ALTERNATE MEASUREMENTS AND UNITS
½ teaspoon		2.5 ml	
1 teaspoon	1/6 oz	5 ml	
½ tablespoon	¼ oz	7.5 ml	1 ½ teaspoons
1 tablespoon	½ oz	15 ml	3 teaspoons
3 tablespoons	1 oz	45 ml	
¼ cup	2 oz	60 ml	4 tablespoons
1/3 cup	2.5 oz	80 ml	
½ cup	4 oz	120 ml	
¾ cup	6 oz	180 ml	
1 cup	8 oz	240 ml	½ pint, ¼ quart
2 cups	16 oz	480 ml	1 pint, ½ quart
4 cups	32 0z	1 L	1 quart, ¼ gallon
16 cups	128 0z	4 L	1 gallon

Weight Equivalents

IMPERIAL	METRIC (ROUNDED)
½ oz	15 g
1 oz	30 g
2 oz	60 g
4 oz	120 g
5 oz	140 g
6 oz	170 g
8 0z	230 g
10 oz	285 g
12 oz	340 g
16 oz/1 lb	450 g
2 lb	900 g

Made in the USA
San Bernardino, CA
13 November 2019